# STRESS-FREE SUSTAINABILITY:
Leverage Your Emotions, Avoid Burnout, and Influence Anyone

ADAM HAMMES

Copyright © 2014 Adam Hammes, ecofluence
All rights reserved. No part of this publication may be reproduced, distributed, or transmitted in any form or by any means, including photocopying, recording, or other electronic or mechanical methods, without the prior written permission of the publisher, except in the case of brief quotations embodied in reviews and certain other non-commercial uses permitted by copyright law
ISBN-13: 978-1508888079
ISBN-10: 1508888078

# EARLY PRAISE FOR STRESS-FREE SUSTAINABILITY

"It's one thing to have numbers. It's another thing to know what to do with them. And the soft stuff – that Adam gives such brilliant guidance to people on – is an incredible set of resources for people trying not to screw this up when they are being led by their passions."

**Bob Willard** – International Speaker, Author of *Sustainability Champion's Guidebook*, *The Next Sustainability Wave*, and *The New Sustainability Advantage*

"Adam has done a fantastic job pulling this all together in a reader-friendly way! It really hit home personally for me. While I implement many parts of what he shares in my life, I was still missing out on some of the anger and arrogance side of getting people to understand. It hits home that he can summarize this information because he 'got it' already from experience, and got it at an age almost thirty years younger than when I got it – today."

**John Cusack** – Senior Manager in Responsible Investment, *Co-founder of Innovest Strategic Advisors, Founder of Gifford Park Associates*

"When I started using the word 'organic' in my lifestyle programs, I surprisingly found that it was a term I was continually having to dance around or say quietly and gingerly. Adam's book has magically awakened my own realization of stress, burnout, and having to defend or justify when I feel confronted. I'm thankful for this wonderful reminder and guide for how to "stick with it," stay influentially true, and at the same time continue to figure out how this organism can better adapt and survive in the current system."

**Michele Beschen** – DIY Media Personality, Business Owner, *Re.Make.Life, b.Organic, b.Original, Courage to Create*

"This beautiful book points to the heart of what hinders my capacity to make a difference - me. Sometimes I stop relating to people as people and I think my agenda is more important than theirs, I lose touch with them and thus lose my ability to make a difference."

**Mike George** - Owner of Cafe Gratitude Kansas City, Software Engineer, *Phenomenons of Consciousness Seminar*

"Adam's book provides world-changers with the tools to cool our passions just enough to build the critical relationships we need to cultivate. It is chock full of concrete strategies, but also great reminders about listening, about love, and about how the power of seeking truth and understanding above "what's right" will help us make the world a better place, together."

**Julie Diegel** – Director of Sustainability Programs, Conference Organizer, *WasteCap Nebraska, Annual Sustainability Summit, "Good Company" Business Training Program*

"As a sustainability professional for over 10 years, I found Adam's perspective on what it means to be human, what motivates people, and how to share my message with others both insightful and liberating. I learned new ways to live and work that are more effortless and life-giving, something I truly appreciate as one who has been to burn-out, and back to balance, in my own sustainability journey. Whether you are just starting your journey into sustainability or have been in it for years, this book will unlock insights into how you do your work. Even more, through profound wisdom and practical exercises, "Stress-Free Sustainability" will give you insight into your own journey and how to celebrate the personal journey of each person you meet to cultivate positive change in your community."

**Daniel Lawse** – Chief Century Thinker, Sustainability Consultant, *Verdis Group, Bio-Inspired Leadership Immersion*

"This book captures the personal evolution that Adam has undergone the past several years in how he engages individuals and groups with sustainability topics. He shares his personal evolution in a way that makes it highly accessible to those of us working in a broad range of areas. *Stress-Free Sustainability* is a treasure trove of insights and resources for people who care about making the world a better place."

**Anthony Thompson** – Sustainability PhD, Sustainable Farmer, *New Family Farm CSA, VP of Iowa Farmers' Union*

"This book is well written, and I could follow the train of thought from one part to the next easily. I was surprised it was such a short, quick read through the first time. I realize now I am the only thing standing in my way. Adam did a very good job of pointing that out without creating a defensive response from me. The change I experienced was immediate. I shocked my 16 year old this morning when I didn't give her a lecture for throwing a recyclable in the trash – I just walked over and moved it and smiled at her since she was telling me a story. I realized that before reading your book I would have interrupted her to teach her a lesson and probably gone off on a lecture about waste in this country – never hearing what she has to say. Instead I got to hear what happened to her yesterday, what she has planned today, and her plans for her future. I may get a dentist in the family, and I never expected that. And I never would have known it was on her mind if I hadn't read this book. Thank you!"

**Samijo Miron** – Public Speaker, Advocate/Activist, *Average Mom, Volunteer Woodland Wildcats Swim Boosters, Skipping Foal Farms*

## DEDICATION

This book is dedicated to my parents, Vernon and Melody.
I couldn't have asked for a better life and it's all thanks to you. I am eternally grateful..

# CONTENTS

Acknowledgments ..... i
Foreword ..... ii
Introduction ..... 1

PART 1 – Leverage Your Emotions ..... 11
    Chapter 1: Threatened ..... 13
    Chapter 2: Invasive ..... 21
    Chapter 3: Keystone ..... 29
    Chapter 4: Avoid Burnout ..... 39

PART 2 – Eliminate Stress ..... 49
    Chapter 5: Contempt ..... 51
    Chapter 6: Curiosity ..... 61
    Chapter 7: Commitment ..... 71

PART 3 – Influence Anyone ..... 83
    Chapter 8: Influence Groups ..... 85
    Chapter 9: Influence Individuals ..... 97

Summary ..... 111
About the Author ..... 115
One Million Minds ..... 117

# ACKNOWLEDGMENTS

A special note of gratitude goes out to all those who made this book possible.

Heroes and mentors who have shaped my own path: I would not be where I am today without the work and encouragement of: Ray Anderson, Bob Willard, Hunter Lovins, Bob Doppelt, and Simran Sethi. Your being in the world has been a gift to me, and so many others.

My writing coaches and friends who didn't listen to my excuses, but pushed me to finish the book concisely and on time: Chandler Bolt, James Roper, and Tyler Wagner. Keep being a stand for passionate people everywhere to get their voice out into the world.

The following, who read an early draft and offered their unfiltered feedback, helped ensure that the content of the book made sense and had practical application in the life of a sustainability professional: John Cusack, Mike Seaman and Samijo Miron. Thank you for your generosity.

My editor extraordinaire, Jill Boniface, for her voice of reason, attention to detail, and ability to work under an extremely tight deadline – I applaud your willpower and your heart. My designer, Niall Gray, for his skill and speed under pressure – without your accuracy on such short notice, this book would never have come together in time.

To the teachers and leaders who have inspired me to do what I love along the way, and do it with integrity: Don Briggs and Kathleen Scholl from the University of Northern Iowa, Travis Langen from the Catalina Environmental Leadership Program, Richard Murphy from Ocean Futures Society, and John Feldman from Kum & Go.

Des Moines advocates who have inspired me or even stood by my side and made every successful project that I've been fortunate enough to participate on possible: the original and current board members for Urban Ambassadors and all the volunteers that show up to improve Des Moines, Ron Sorenson and Gary Monte from KFMG 99.1 FM for the "Green City" segment, Lynnae Hentzen and Chaden Halfhill from Center on Sustainable Communities for your leadership, and countless others in their offices, neighborhoods, families, and homes making a difference every day.

And to the thousands of social and environmental pioneers that have come before me, and the millions that will come after. It is an honor to be in this work with you. You have my undying appreciation.

# FOREWORD

There are some amazing people in this world working wholeheartedly to make a difference on so many levels, and Adam Hammes is one of those people. I first met Adam a few years ago when he was the manager of sustainability for a locally-based corporation. We've naturally stayed on each other's radar through some of our like-minded efforts.

When he asked me to write a foreword for his book, it triggered a more inward look at my own relationship with 'sustainability' over the years and the role each of us play in leaving this world a bit better than we found it. These roles are as unique as the individuals orchestrating them. This book shows us how to better utilize our distinctive gifts, resources, connections, and – ultimately -- the conscious choices we are making each day to make that difference.

My role has always been one of sharing ideas and stories in a way that helps people get excited about how they can take action in their own backyards. I believe it truly starts at home with each and every one of us in how we are actively living our lives, so I love how Adam's words and directives are all about taking action in sensible, relatable ways. This book has compelled me to take a deeper look at community and connection in ways that take what we are doing at home, and in our own backyards, and ignites something even more collective and with greater impact. As I read through the pages, there were many of my own "Aha" moments where I was thinking "YES, I've felt like that!" and "Phew, I'm not the only one," and "Dang, if I'd only had some of these exercises earlier, maybe I could have been a bit more effective in how I navigated similar experiences and opportunities"! For me personally, reading this book reminded me of my own emotional struggles with working from the heart.

I saw how my personal attachment to the overall mission made it difficult for me to compromise in some of the more effective, influential ways that Adam writes about.

When I started using the word 'organic' in my lifestyle programs, I surprisingly found that it was a term that I was continually having to dance around or speak of quietly and gingerly. This book magically awakened my own realization of stress, burnout, and having to defend or justify when I feel confronted. I now have the tools that Adam so thoughtfully packages up in this book to still work from the heart, but in a more impactful, sustainable way.

Caring deeply about something goes even farther when you combine it with the usable framework that he has so generously made available to all of us. Adam asks us the questions that he has asked of himself, which makes this book refreshingly honest and revealing. It's in this authenticity that we eagerly and openly answer those inquisitions for ourselves, allowing us to get even more out of the practical exercises and other beneficial resources he provides. I know I am incredibly grateful for this wonderful reminder and guide for how to "stick with it," stay influentially true, and at the same time continue to figure out how this organism can better adapt and survive in the current system.

It's not another preachy book about sustainability that makes you feel even more overwhelmed, confused, and small. It's a book that puts YOU and YOUR ROLE at the forefront of it all. Read vigorously and enjoy!

**Michele Beschen**
Lifestyle Instructor, TV Personality, Artisan,
Speaker on Creativity & Natural Living
*Remake.Life, B. Organic, B. Original,*
*Michele Beschen's Courage to Create*
March 17, 2015
Des Moines, Iowa

# INTRODUCTION

*"Be the change you want to see in the world."*
~ Mahatma Ghandi

You want to make a difference. You want your life to be a meaningful contribution to the world – your community, your workplace, and your friends and family. Otherwise, you wouldn't be reading this introduction, let alone this book.

Your passions face difficult circumstances: conflicting views, argumentative opposition, and emotional ups and downs. You probably meet various obstacles regularly, and you may have experienced burnout on multiple occasions.

Possibly, you've even contemplated giving up – giving up on causes in which you believe strongly, and for which you have a real passion. Who knows? Maybe you've already quit, and this little book is your last-ditch effort to rekindle a fire you never wanted to go out.

If it makes you feel any better, I know what you're going through.

You made a good choice giving this book a chance. I have no doubts that this short read will forever change you, and your experience of feeling stopped when you're up to big things. It might be what frees you from a vicious cycle of frustration and burnout – the exhaustion of advocacy.

I have no doubts because I am writing this book for myself.

I need a friendly reminder when my own blind spots slow me down. I am writing it because I still need to hear it, again and again. When I get distracted from the truth, and just plain tired, I need to remember these powerful ideas from mentors, heroes, and friends who have taught me so much.

These pages pull me out of the mud – the limiting beliefs rampant in our field. They completely transform my ability to successfully champion the change I want see in the world.

And, you know what? I believe the world needs me. And if it needs someone like me, then it most certainly needs you.

## The State of the World

I'm not going to sugarcoat things. This book is not about the power of positive thinking. There are real problems facing all corners of our society and our planet.

- Continuous war
- Indentured servitude
- Child labor
- Sex trade
- Water pollution
- Air pollution
- Soil loss
- Hazardous working conditions
- Non-living wages
- Job shortages
- Food shortages
- Floods
- Droughts
- Loss of biodiversity
- Water shortages
- Ocean desalinization
- Coral reef bleaching
- Fisheries collapse
- Wildlife extinction
- Climate destabilization

This is an overwhelming list.

It can paralyze people when they first see it and begin to comprehend the realities around the globe. Some try to deny these problems exist. I will be the first to admit that both sides of the media and politics exaggerate and sensationalize each issue for their own ends. However, each item on the list also has its own wealth of documented scientific evidence.

Which brings me to the reason why this book is so important.

### The Problem with Facts

When it comes to making a difference in the world, evidence is only as valuable as the way in which it is communicated – by those who know and understand it, to those who don't.

Said another way: Facts, delivered poorly, are facts to very few people.

Solutions exist for the issues facing our planet and society. Rooted in leadership, technology, and healthy alternatives, they are out there.

It's not from a lack of facts or research or data that these problems still exist in the world. But you may be using that as an excuse not to act. I urge you to reconsider.

In Frances Moore Lappe's book Eco Mind, she writes, "As the economic crisis hit in 2009, four in ten Americans still ranked the environment as a top priority. Just a few years ago, nearly 80 percent of us said we were 'ready to make significant changes to the way [we] live to reduce climate impact.' And about 70 percent of people polled in twenty-one countries agreed."

Consider this. If millions of people understand and believe we should change, why aren't we?

Because these millions of people are not necessarily in positions of authority to make key decisions. Still, they are the only ones qualified to convince those who are in positions of authority and decision-making of what needs to be done. Those who don't understand the issues, or believe that no solutions exist, can't be expected to convince themselves.

We don't need to master the facts – the data – about our problems. We have enough facts and data.

We need influence.

We need to supplement our facts with a healthy dose of psychology and behavior change. We need to learn to recognize the stages of influence individuals must go through, and strategies that help them along their journey. We need to master the art and science of persuasion to motivate those who don't know and understand the facts.

In the words of Hunter Lovins, "It's our job to get better at talking to them."

And you can. That is what this book supplies. In the next hour or two you can literally change what you know is possible. Read on.

## What Do I Know?

An introvert by nature, I have always had an insatiable desire to escape into books. Over the past 15 years I've digested hundreds of them – many good, many not that helpful. When I struggled, which was often, I would force myself to venture out of my shell to ask questions so I could figure out what I was doing wrong.

In one particular stroke of luck, in 2008, I was being interviewed on a local radio program and the ex-mayor offered that I host my own segment on sustainability. Through that opportunity alone, I ended up interviewing over 200 leaders I greatly admired, and was able to ask them what strategies worked for them.

I am also eternally grateful to have met visionaries like Hunter Lovins, Ray Anderson, Bob Willard, and Simran Sethi, who set me on a different path than when I began.

They shook me from my strictly fact-based pursuits of sustainability and introduced me to an entirely new body of knowledge. They saved me from burnout and helped me eliminate stress with the latest research on emotional intelligence, social psychology, green marketing, and change management. And that has made all the difference.

You could say that I've borrowed and tested everything I could over the past 15 years to see what would work for me and why. And because I can be a bit of a workaholic, I boiled it down to an easy-to-use framework to save myself time. I made it as simple and easy-to-understand as possible so I could get the majority of my introvert ideas out of my head and into the world. Today, I spend my time helping organizations and individuals do the same.

## What to Expect

If you Know Your Self, Know Your Strategy, and Know Your Audience – and build practices around each – those three things will be the key to making a huge shift in your ability to make the difference you are out to make in the world.

After even one hour of reading this short book of stories, concepts, and techniques, you'll have the insight and inspiration you've been looking for. I've made sure to include Critical Questions to ask yourself after each section, Practical Exercises to help you gain experience, and Additional Resources that will help you dig deeper in areas you feel necessary.

Dozens of new approaches to championing sustainability will be at your service, from the way you speak, to the way you write, to the way you approach problems in your family, office and city. You will be able to take on more than one complex issue at a time. You will be able to tailor a unique and stage-appropriate strategy for each one.

You will understand and be able to recognize that individuals you speak to have their own perspective to consider when framing your communication. No more of the right idea at the wrong time. No more one-size-fits-all. No more wasting your precious time and energy on people you don't need to influence, but to whom you've been giving away your power.

This isn't conjecture or guessing.

Maybe you're an introvert and can resonate with the extra work I needed to put in to make the soft skills a priority. If you're a natural and love interacting with people, with this framework you'll move much faster than I did.

Regardless, the best thing I can share with you is my story and let you know that my journey was fraught with speed bumps, false starts, and full stops. I am confident that by learning from my mistakes, you will be capable of achieving your own dreams faster than me.

# The Proof is in the Pudding

In college, I earned a minor in environmental studies and worked as an environmental educator, a leadership trainer, and then an outreach coordinator for a world-renowned sustainability program. I earned my Master's degree studying social and environmental business, became adjunct faculty at university, founded a grassroots non-profit, and started launching initiatives in my city with other passionate residents.

We started a local Transition Town group. We created a sustainable spring break for college and high school students. We recreated a famous transportation photo from Germany and made it available to the world for marketing campaigns.

We started school gardens, brought in green CEOs to speak to business leaders, and designed pop-up parks in Park(ing) Day spaces downtown. We created an annual conference that brought together the local food and hunger fighting communities. And we started a group micro-lending program for women in poverty modeled after Grameen Bank.

I became the manager of sustainability for a corporation with $3 billion in revenue. After three and a half years, I quit to become a sustainability consultant working for multiple companies, a state-wide initiative, and local community projects. I started getting invited to speak at conferences and coach other sustainability professionals. Today, as I write this, I'm working on a campaign for online video-training for a garden at every school and bringing together two sides of a heated water quality debate in our state.

At age 33, I have done some things that I feel very good about.

It is a part of my personality that I worry you'll think I'm full of myself sharing even those three paragraphs with you – that I'll sound arrogant and craving of attention. True, I want you to have some background on me. I want you to know there is value in these pages from real-world experience, not just theory. But attention is far from what I crave.

The attention should go to the following pages. And to the many sources that I've drawn from over my lifetime. Many books have been written, and many conversations and training have been enjoyed, that shaped my mindset and this content. I've merely re-organized it here for you in the simplest and clearest way I know possible. My goal was to write a 100-page book that could change the world. I may have gone a bit over, but you'll find that throughout these pages I give credit to those who came before me, as well as direct you to additional resources for more depth, if desired.

When I got asked to speak at my first conference, the idea terrified me. I knew the framework I used to get where I am. I knew the strategies I chose and why.

But standing up and telling other people to do the same thing was frightening. I like to work behind the scenes.

I envisioned having to make bold declarations and being confronted with, "Oh, yeah. Well, that might have worked for you, but what about my issue? It's not the same thing!" All that in front of a crowd of 200 people? I'd rather chew on tin foil.

I agreed before I even knew what I was supposed to talk about. The incredible amount of discomfort I felt was surely a sign that this was a growth opportunity. In the months leading up to the conference, I wrestled with how to proceed. Late one night, stressing over how to present my success stories, I had an epiphany of sorts.

You don't care about my success stories. You only want to know if I can help you have your own success stories, and how. Strangely, that was a huge relief. It was no longer about me.

So I scrapped most of my presentation and focused on two things: (1) the emotions I dealt with working on different projects, and (2) providing opportunities for the audience to share their own similar stories. Because I shared the human side of my own trials and tribulations, people opened up. The whole room learned more than I could ever teach.

Today, I continue to force myself to share personal stories – my own and those others have shared with me – for one reason only. It helps people more than anything else.

Despite how vulnerable it makes me feel as an introvert, I now know that my stories, and yours, are the most powerful tools we possess. They help us connect and relate to one another. They help us see ourselves in the stories of others.

Your stories are what make you uniquely qualified to transform your community in ways that I never could. So, really, I only tell my stories in the hope that you'll be inspired to embrace your own.

## What's the Worst That Could Happen?

If you don't read this book, or make an effort to learn this content somewhere else, nothing terrible will happen. Nothing new will happen, either.

Things will stay the same for you.

Things stayed the same for me in my early 20s. I worked hard on initiatives I believed in, and gained little or no traction at the scale I wanted. I failed often, but failure isn't terrible. It can be a great teacher.

Consider that passion, like willpower, starts strong but will fade over time. If you continue to fall short of your goals, it leads to cynicism – about the world, your co-workers and bosses, and even your own ability to make a difference.

If you have damaged relationships in the past, you will logically continue to damage future relationships for the same reasons until you try something new. You will grow more frustrated with those you believe should change. And, as I contemplated doing several times, if you don't find a new approach you will eventually quit.

When I thought about quitting, I wanted to blame other people for my frustration. Exasperated, I would tell myself, "Why even try? Nothing's going to change. It's hopeless." And in a way I was right.

It was not because other people weren't listening to me. That was only a symptom of my problem. The cause was that I had chosen to take a severely limited approach to change. I was capable of leading in a variety of different ways, and I was stubbornly using the same approach every time.

The world needed me to be better – to learn and grow. Just like the world needs you to learn and grow. The world desperately needs you to contribute your unique and special gifts – the ones that you, and only you, can contribute. It needs you to make a difference by expanding what is possible, to literally help save the planet. And that is no exaggeration.

## Guaranteed to Satisfy

This little book will completely shift how you look at making a difference. It will make the world feel like a simpler place. You will notice things you've never noticed, and you'll realize that things you have noticed in the past are actually the clues you've been hoping for. They are the keys to your success.

Try on the new perspectives in these short pages. You will be able to practice influence techniques that seem effortless in comparison to what you're accustomed. You will find yourself working less and accomplishing more.

You will be happier, have more energy, and build relationships you never thought possible.

Your circle of influence will expand. Your confidence will soar, as you tackle larger and larger issues where you feel called to contribute. And you will build larger and larger coalitions in your community to enact change.

You know what's even better?

As you and others share these simple strategies with more change agents around the world, the ripple effect will touch every corner of the earth. You will wake up and not recognize the world in a few years. It will be teeming with revitalized communities across the globe. And it will be, in no small part, thanks to you.

## What Change Do You Want to See?

Can you envision a world where passion and caring are constantly being translated into powerful action?

Can you picture socially- and environmentally-conscious people around the world having high-impact conversations that produce amazing results in their communities?

If that's a stretch, try it now.

Close your eyes and visualize what it would be like. Imagine yourself and twenty other visionary leaders in your city. See them having real conversations throughout their day – on the phone, around the table, in a meeting, at a coffee shop, in front of a crowd – and people are listening. The message is getting through. Those who you expect to argue, shut down, or turn off are showing interest. Those from whom you expect mild support are making commitments and taking action. And the visionary leaders – that's you – are generating meaningful change more rapidly than they ever thought possible.

If you can hold that vivid scene in your mind, I invite you to join me in what I'm calling the One Million Minds campaign. It's my vision that we can help one million passionate people around the world leverage their emotions, avoid burnout, eliminate stress, and influence anyone. All this to move, inspire, and transform our communities, one by one, creating a tipping point for the planet. Together, I believe we can do that – One Million Minds strong.

If you bought the print version of this book, you've already contributed by donating $1 to two organizations ensuring that the next generation understands sustainability: Net Impact and AASHE (Association for the Advancement of Sustainability in Higher Education). These two organizations are helping our next generation participate in solving the critical social and environmental issues of this generation.

Just the fact that you're still reading says a lot about who you are. In some fashion, you rearranged your day. You've carved out time for a short read, but for a specific purpose that will benefit the world. So, I applaud you simply for making it this far. Thank you for what you're up to in life. We need people like you.

You may be a passionate resident, a concerned parent, or an engaged college student. Maybe you design socially- and environmentally-responsible products and services or try to improve your office environment. Maybe you're a caring business owner, a social entrepreneur, or serve in a regulatory position. Whatever your arena, you are playing a big game and this new playbook has a lot to offer your journey to success.

## How to Get the Most Out of This Book

I want to be clear before we start.

You know more about your passion than I ever will. You are the expert in the room, not me. So, you have to bring what you care about most into this conversation.

Yes, you are going to be learning a practical, easy-to-use framework. Yes, you will hear stories and experiences from my journey and the journeys of others like you. But these will only provide you with a fraction of the value you can expect if you insert your mission along the way.

What will that look like?

What will provide an incredible amount of value to you?

You have to be willing to bring up areas where you feel stuck. You have to ask yourself and honestly answer the Critical Questions dotted throughout the chapters. You have to do the Practical Exercises at the end of the chapters, applying what you've read to your own cause.

Scribble notes as you read: capture passages that resonate with you, capture passages that make you uncomfortable. Share with a colleague. Get an accountability partner. Start a book club.

There will be some chapters where you feel really strong in the skills and practices discussed. In other chapters, you may evaluate yourself as needing more work in that area. That's great. Dive deeper with the Additional Resources provided.

I encourage you to think about and observe moments when you are already using some of the suggestions in the book. Celebrate the little things. Because they become the big things. Don't be too hard on yourself. I'm here to point out ways in which we struggle, but that doesn't mean life and advocacy is only struggle. For all the ways things go right, I recommend reading my blog at www.eco-fluence.com, including a post from January 3, 2014 called Spend Time with Your Eco-Heroes.

Don't just skim through these pages and check it off your list. This isn't a contest to read the most books.

This is your chance to change your life and what's possible in an area you care deeply about. So, do the work that will get you unstuck on something that matters to you. My promise is to walk through new concepts with you, tell stories, and offer different ways of looking at existing problems you face. I'm here with you to provide a breakthrough experience with breakthrough results – your own personal "Aha!" moment.

This book is a guide to help you see new ways to take action, be more effective, and get what you want where it means the most to you.

That's it. No big deal, right? Then let's get started.

PART 1
## LEVERAGE YOUR EMOTIONS

*"All we need to know is that feelings are important, that we each have all of them, and that it is healthy to begin to know them and to talk about them."*
~ Charles L. Whitfield

This book has something for everyone. And that's because at our core, we're all emotional beings. Our feelings have a very personal flavor, yet we all have feelings. They connect us at the level of universal experience.

You may not understand exactly how it felt for me when I was four years old and found out that my brother had brain damage because of an unlicensed anesthesiologist. And that he would never have a normal childhood and life like other kids. But you've been confused. You know what it feels like to be sad and angry. And you've had to watch people that you love and care about suffer.

You may not understand exactly how it felt for me when I was 28 years old and organized my first event that brought over one hundred advocates out on a steaming hot summer day (103 degrees Fahrenheit). But you've been proud. You know the courage it takes to try something new. And you've beamed with joy at life's little surprises.

I don't have a monopoly on strong feelings. No one does. But if you can leverage them in a healthy manner, they hold the secret to maximizing your impact in the world.

Here's how. Know Your Self.

On our journey of emotional maturity, there are two common over-corrections that occur on the way to healthy emotional intelligence: (1) suppressing our emotions, and (2) reacting to our emotions.

In actuality, our emotions are our indicators that we have an opportunity for either growth or expression.

They can leave us feeling weak. They can leave us feeling strong. Sometimes they are helpful and we can trust them to guide us into action and contribution. Sometimes they are less helpful and we can trust them to guide us into reaction and apology. Later, as we reflect on our emotions and what we chose to do with them, there are real lessons for growth.

Either way, emotions are an amazing form of communication our subconscious mind and body has with our conscious mind and body.

They are truly fascinating gifts. Best not to meet them with suppression or reaction, but with attention and consideration.

In these next three chapters, I'm going to share stories with you that illustrate a powerful way to recognize and move quickly through these two over-corrections. I'm going to share my own stories and those of other passionate individuals who I've coached or who have shared at my talks.

Your own journey of emotional maturity is really the only one I want you to care about. Take the time to reflect and see if you can see yourself in any of these stories.

Although emotional intelligence is a complex topic, a huge thank you goes out to Keith Summerville, professor of environmental science and policy at Drake University, for hammering out ecological metaphors for the major concepts that would resonate vividly with social and environmental advocates everywhere. Enjoy.

## CHAPTER 1
## **THREATENED**

*"I learned that courage was not the absence of fear, but the triumph over it. The brave man is not he who does not feel afraid, but he who conquers that fear."*
~ Nelson Mandela

In 1980, I was born in a small county hospital in Washington, Iowa. The town had approximately seven thousand people, but only because it was the county seat. Being in the southeastern portion of the state, it was still half an hour from Iowa City – a whopping seventy thousand people.

My own hometown of Richland was too small (population 400) to have a hospital. I was raised on a beautiful little acreage five miles north of town, on a double dead-end road. Our farmhouse was on a hill overlooking the woods on the South Skunk River. The summers were humid and lush green – full of chirping crickets and hungry mosquitoes. The winters were frigid and powder-white with snow – deathly quiet.

Picture me, an ornery little eleven-year-old who loved being outside and playing in the dirt. I would camp by the river, hike in the woods, and walk the fence rows and stream beds around our family's property with my older sister, younger brother, cousins and friends. I had two classmates who lived within a few miles and would visit on ATVs. Occasionally we would ride our horses across the river to visit relatives.

Dad raised all kinds of animals while we were growing up: chickens, goats, sheep, pigs, hunting dogs, quail and even ostriches for a few odd years. Mom, a special kind of angel, worked with special needs children and adults. We didn't have much, but we worked hard and got by.

My parents both came from large Catholic families. My dad's family had fifteen children, all of whom worked on their farm growing up. My mom's parents divorced and each had five children in their respective families. Aunts and uncles and cousins were in abundance. We certainly had enough for two teams at any sport when it came to family reunions.

Richland was and still is a small farming community. On the odd occasions when I did sit down to watch the news, it was the local station. As far I could tell George H. W. Bush was president.

At eleven I wasn't very political, but it seemed to me like there was a lot wrong with the world. The first Gulf War was under way, and the conversation at our house was of a conservative nature, to say the least.

My favorite movie was the Swiss Family Robinson. I felt that if the world was in such bad shape, what better way to spend life than far away from society on a desert island with only the ones you love. Having a kick-ass treehouse and riding around on ostriches sounded all right to me, too.

Our neighbors farmed the fields of seed corn and soy beans surrounding our acreage. Soon they began combatting their economic struggles by maximizing yields per acre. For me, that just meant that hundreds of trees were being bulldozed along my favorite fence lines and stream beds for a few extra rows of crops. The dead remains were piled high, left as an ugly reminder that I used to be able to play there.

I didn't get into hunting. I enjoyed books more than guns. I liked art. Fishing not so much. And I thought that people needed to treat each other, animals and the planet, with a lot more respect. I was eleven when I first remember hearing the word "environmentalist" on TV. I knew I was one. And that scared me. It certainly was not used in a positive way in our family. It definitely did not feel okay to be one. In fact, I was convinced at that age the only thing more disappointing for my family would be if I was gay.

So, there I was – eleven and didn't feel safe sharing who I was or how I felt. I was afraid to express how frustrated I was about things I saw happening in the world. I was sad because I thought my family would be disappointed if I told them the truth. So in my mind, I chose survival. I bottled it up. I felt scared to be seen as different – to not fit in – and grief that apparently I had to deal with it on my own.

That's what it can be like to feel threatened – lonely, weak, unsafe, afraid, and sad.

### Critical Questions

- What is your earliest memory of feeling threatened?
- How old were you? Where were you?
- What happened? What did you tell yourself about the situation?
- Did you make it mean something about who you were?
- Did you say "Something's wrong" or "I'm not good enough"?

### The Polar Bear – Part 1

Today, nine out of eighteen subpopulations of polar bears (Ursus maritimus) are in decline. Ecologically speaking, they have a limited and shrinking number of places where they can thrive. Adapted to a narrow ecological niche, a polar bear's range is almost exclusively within the Arctic Circle.

External influences of climate change, oil and gas development, and pollution – things beyond their control – are undermining their ability to reproduce. And so they've become symbolic in the environmental community as a victim of negative human impacts on our planet.

When you think of a polar bear, you might picture one perched precariously on a melting chunk of ice surrounded by freezing water – a desperate look on its face. Or maybe you think of the popular 2011 Nissan commercial, walking thousands of miles to hug a new Leaf owner in their driveway.

Either way, what kind of emotional reaction do you feel?

Seeing such a powerful animal unable to defend itself is a bit heartbreaking for me.

I can relate. And that's why I love to use the story of the polar bear when I speak at conferences. It's a powerful metaphor for the emotional state many passionate people in the world experience. They feel threatened by their surroundings, and unable to be fully self-expressed – unable to thrive.

If you feel threatened, you are one step away from being endangered, and possibly becoming extinct. Your ability to be effective in the world is largely limited by your surroundings. This will cause a serious lack of confidence. Giving up on your passion out of frustration is a real possibility.

Threatened people burn out quickly.

At age eleven, the environmentalist in me felt threatened. And I probably would have it let it become extinct. But high school ended, and I moved a couple of hours away to college.

Fast forward. In 2008, while hosting a local radio program, I began interviewing people I admired and looked up to – leaders and community members doing meaningful work in the city. I wanted to learn what they did to get where they were today.

I asked questions about their journey. I asked questions about their lessons learned.

But I also asked questions like, "What is your number one frustration?" and "What keeps you up at night worrying?"

I wanted to hear what they were still struggling with even though I looked up to them as a success story. Where were they stopped or stuck?

The answers surprised me. And they made me realize I wasn't alone in my own struggles.

Highly-intelligent professionals with good careers and a wealth of knowledge on sustainability topics were still frustrated. Often it was with close family and business relationships where they didn't feel heard or understood. They felt resigned that they couldn't talk about their beliefs with loved ones. They felt sad colleagues who were in a position to make a difference didn't seem to care.

And they felt frustrated and afraid that some of their big visions kept meeting with resistance and might not be realized.

Sara was a senior environmental studies major and planner for an annual sustainability conference. She confessed to being burnt out already, and was wondering if she should consider pursuing another career. Was sustainability really catching on or was it all wishful thinking? Her efforts in college clubs and with a local non-profit had produced lack-luster results, in her opinion. She felt the issues got overlooked too easily by administrators and the business community.

Tonya was a board member in her forties. A teacher and actress, she worked hard to make a difference with her students and for local organizations. She described the sinking feeling she got whenever her older sister would make condescending comments about her passions. "Does that Prius come standard with an Obama sticker?" Or "I thought you might bring something weird," at the family dinner to justify why she brought an extra dish for everyone. Her neighbors were pushy and complained about their property values because she didn't want to put vinyl siding on her house. As a single mom, she worried first about giving her two sons the life they deserved, and also about living a life in line with her values.

Steven was a friend in his forties and owner of a green building firm. He didn't believe his own employees were buying into his environmental vision for the company. He didn't know what to do and it frustrated him at night thinking about it. At home, he and his wife were also struggling with their in-laws, not feeling supported with the choices they were making to raise healthy children. It was exhausting for him. He worried about his own health and wellness.

His passion kept him going, but he sometimes felt like he was running on fumes.

There are so many stories just like this.

You are not alone.

## Threatened Emotions

Children aren't the only ones who feel threatened. Even as an adult and a professional you face times when you still feel lonely, afraid, sad or unsafe. You wrestle with choosing safety and survival – fitting in – over sharing how you really feel and the risk of not being accepted.

Difficult emotions like shame, guilt, fear, and sadness are a natural part of daily life. They can make you feel weak, but ideally, you will find healthy ways to express those emotions at appropriate times and be that much better off for it.

It becomes problematic when a particular difficult emotion becomes a way of life – your emotional center of gravity.

Moments of loneliness, fear, or sadness can become weeks, months, or even years. When that happens, it becomes very easy to stay frustrated, overwhelmed, and burn out. One common coping mechanism for this problem is suppression.

You learn as a child that it is possible, and sometimes encouraged, to suppress difficult emotions. As a temporary coping mechanism, this can be highly effective for you. But if you don't deal with the root cause, and you adopt suppression as a way of life, disassociating from your emotions is stunting. It will hurt your ability to form healthy relationships and to fully experience joy.

---

**Practical Exercises**

Find at least one other passionate change agent in your community that you feel comfortable sharing with. Ask them to read this book with you, and do these exercises. If you really want a breakthrough in your community, invite a large group of community leaders to participate in a book club with you. Give each person five minutes to share the answers to the following questions with each other:
- Where today do you feel afraid or unable to openly share your passion?
- When do you feel stopped in sharing your true thoughts and feelings?
- Have you ever been frustrated to the point you considered giving up on your mission or passion? Be honest.

---

### The Polar Bear – Part 2

Earlier I shared that nine out of eighteen subpopulations of polar bears are in decline. What I didn't share was that they are not categorized by the International Union for the Conservation of Nature as "threatened." Technically, they are only "vulnerable," which means they will become threatened if their situation doesn't change.

Polar bears are incredibly resilient creatures, with up to ten inches of hide and fur to insulate them from the cold. Although vulnerable, these thick-skinned powerhouses are also the largest land predators in the world – larger even than their cousin, the Kodiak. With a keen sense of smell, hearing, and eyesight, the polar bear is nothing to be messed with. It is no coincidence that polar bears have historically been a spiritual and cultural symbol of strength to native northern tribes.

There are real dangers that exist for the polar bear as a species – things beyond their control. Yet the truth behind those desperate photos is that we sometimes project our own emotions onto animals. If current conservation efforts continue – financial, legislative, and educational – polar bears have a real shot at survival. And, if you ever see one in the wild, don't worry about their safety and how they're doing. Seek shelter.

## Vulnerable versus Threatened

As typically happens when I think of a clever metaphor, people poke holes in it immediately. I was speaking at a sustainability summit for the recycling industry and a state representative stood up and shared with the room.

"Just last month I was a polar bear, and damn proud, too! My daughter got married and I was stuck in a car with her husband and new father-in-law for six hours. He kept talking about Obama this and liberals that. How environmental problems were a big conspiracy. I felt threatened, and it took everything I had not to share how I really felt. But I did it anyway. Because I love my daughter, and it wasn't about how I felt – it was her day."

Amen.

I hope you never believe that just because you're quiet, reserved, or don't speak your mind I think you are doing something wrong – or being ineffective.

The key to leveraging your emotions to avoid burnout and eliminate stress is being able to answer "Yes" to the following questions.

### Critical Questions

- Do you feel like you have the freedom to choose?
- Does reflecting on your interaction leave you feeling good about your choice?

When I was eleven, it didn't feel like a choice. I believed that my options were (1) shut up and fit in, or (2) disappoint my family forever.

When the state senator shut up, he made a conscious choice – and for a valid reason. His daughter's new father-in-law was probably not essential to his personal cause. So, arguing with him during a six-hour ride in a small car would not have furthered that cause. It only would have made things incredibly awkward, if not torturous, for everyone – especially his daughter on her special day.

Feeling threatened isn't experienced as a choice. Being vulnerable is a choice. And you get to choose who you are vulnerable with.

Vulnerability is not "being brutally honest." Too often, that is a smokescreen for wanting to blurt out whatever you're thinking at a particular moment – with no regard for the other person's well-being. Tactlessness. We'll cover this strategy more in the next chapter.

Vulnerability is also not a behind-the-scenes look at your intimate personal life with someone who barely knows you. It's not a tell-all blog, a too-much-information Facebook post, or dumping your feelings, unfiltered, onto a startled stranger.

Real vulnerability is earned. It is sharing difficult emotions like loneliness, fear, or sadness – sometimes even shame or guilt – with someone you trust. It is opening up in a safe environment with another human being who gets you. You need people who have put in the time to demonstrate that they will honor what you have to say.

Real vulnerability is having thick skin when you need to, but finding the time later that day or week to express yourself with a loved one. In that way, you can avoid suppressing your emotions and build stronger relationships at the same time. Only then can you get the help you need to process your emotions in a healthy way for optimal personal growth.

---

**Practical Exercises**

Spend five minutes each sharing the answers to the following questions (with another human being you know and trust):
- What is one area in life where you already choose your battles wisely?
- In what other areas do you see that you have a choice, and could leverage your emotions more successfully?
- Do you have people in your life that you can be vulnerable with? Who are they? How do you feel about them?

---

## Additional Resources

- **Daring Greatly** (book) by Brene Brown
- **The Dark Side of the Light Chasers** (book) by Debbie Ford
- **Transcending the Levels of Consciousness** (book) by David R. Hawkins
- **The Forum** (weekend workshop) by Landmark Education
- **Meditation** (in general) – Disclaimer: I spent 10 years using meditation as an emotional suppression exercise. Be clear that your goal isn't to deny your emotions and thoughts but to notice them and let them go on the cushion. That way, you can get better at noticing and processing them when you're off the cushion.

## CHAPTER 2
## INVASIVE

*"For every minute you remain angry, you give up sixty seconds of peace of mind."*
~ Ralph Waldo Emerson

Class of 1999, I had a full-ride academic scholarship two hours from home at the University of Northern Iowa. I guess one benefit of turning inward as a child was that I excelled in school – a polar bear silver lining. As an introvert, UNI was the perfect compromise. Everything on campus was a fifteen minute walk away, the class sizes were small, and six friends were also going – 13 percent of my graduating class.

If something big hadn't happened, I would have stayed in my shell forever. I majored in management information systems because I liked computer programming. It seemed like being rich would allow me to do whatever I wanted after college. I took twenty credit hours per semester, a part-time job at the cafeteria, and my studies way too seriously. My high school sweetheart (part of that 13 percent) didn't drink, so neither did I. You could often find me in the dormitory lounge until midnight. I got As.

I got As, until Clint Sieren died in a motorcycle accident second semester.

He was one of my best friends in high school and not part of that 13 percent. He went to a college two hours away, but in a different direction. My world just stopped for a few months.

I wasn't the kind of person who planned for the future. My plans were simple: a house near Clint (aka "Chewy") and Matt Askew so we could hang out on nights and weekends. We were going to have big yards so our families could spend time together, then grow old and die happy.

Now what was I supposed to do?

I had been fairly numb already, and this only made things worse. After sleepwalking through the summer, a switch kind of flipped inside my head. I stopped feeling lonely and sad. I started to feel pretty damn angry.

First, I was angry at Clint for dying. But then I was angry at myself for all the times I wasn't there for him. I was angry at my relationship and ended it, two years deep. I was angry at my business professors for dismissing environmental and social issues that mattered to me, so I changed my major.

I was angry at my career choice, so I turned down a lucrative summer internship in Texas. Instead, I went to Okinawa, Japan to teach kids how to swim for $22 per day. It was the only Swiss Family Robinson escape from reality I could find.

There, I found something that felt slightly better than anger – pride.

In a self-centered way, I started to feel a strength that I hadn't felt before. I loved – I mean really loved – traveling and being adventurous. For the first time, I felt comfortable sharing a very real part of who I was. Not only was it accepted, but it was often admired. And pride felt good for someone who was used to being sad and lonely.

When I got back from Okinawa, I took a job teaching rock climbing and leading outdoor adventure trips – hiking, caving, whitewater rafting. I jumped around between different social and environmental causes on campus. Being adventurous helped me find my voice – or at least a voice. And that voice was often arrogant.

Invasively pointing out my own opinions, and things I thought were wrong, became my new way of life.

In 2002, I wrote a two-page email from Chico State in California to my family complaining about George W. Bush and the new war in Iraq. In 2003, I wrote a form letter to the YMCA Camp Erdman in Hawaii complaining that its organizational structure and strategic direction were preventing us from growing. It went on and on like that. I was a real treat to be around. And it made me angry that my insightfulness did not change people's minds. No one listened. My only solace was that I could feel proud that at least I knew the truth, even if they didn't.

That's what it can be like to over-correct in the opposite direction – angry, proud, and invasive.

### Critical Questions

- What is your earliest memory of speaking out and feeling angry when no one listened?
- How old were you? Where were you?
- What happened? What did you tell yourself about the situation?
- Did you make it mean something about those who didn't listen?
- Did you say "Something's wrong" or "They're not good enough"?

### The Killer Bee – Part 1

Killer bees are a hybrid of the Western honey bee (Apis mellifera). An invasive species, they enter existing hives and install their own queen, becoming hyper-protective. The fun characteristics of a killer bee swarm are as follows: they defend a larger radius around their hive, are quicker to swarm, sting a greater number of times, and will chase an intruder over longer distances than typical honey bees.

When you think of a killer bee, you might picture a news anchor pointing to a map of South America with large arrows branching out across the continent – up into Mexico and the southwestern United States. Or maybe you think of that heart-breaking scene in the movie My Girl when Thomas J. tries to find Vada's mood ring and gets stung to death.

Either way, what kind of emotional reaction do you feel? I hear an ominous buzzing and it makes me want to cover any bare skin and run for the hills.

I know that's how my family and the YMCA felt. I've asked them. I love to use the story of the killer bee when I speak at conferences, but for the opposite reason as the polar bear. It's a powerful metaphor for the emotional state others feel when they are around passionate people being led by anger and pride. And it offers priceless insight into the cause of so much frustration we passion-pushers can experience.

If you swing away from fear and sadness to feeling angry and proud, you may feel justified being invasive. After all, you've spent all this time not speaking up; you've got some catching up to do. This can cause a serious case of over-confidence, and you are at risk of reacting instantaneously to your own emotions. Throwing your passion in other people's face is a possible result of this over-correction. And invasive people turn others off instantly.

In college, the environmentalist in me became invasive. And I turned off a lot of people who would have otherwise been interested in what I had to say. Luckily, I eventually met some amazing mentors who helped steer me in another direction.

Fast forward. In 2011, I got asked to coach another sustainability professional for the first time. I didn't feel qualified to be a coach. I did, however, have a deep desire to see this person succeed. My hope was that not a single passionate change agent would ever get frustrated and give up. We truly need you, and a million more like you.

In learning how to coach others, I began to connect the dots between the lessons I heard in my radio interviews and what other professionals were experiencing. The logical next step for people who struggled in the past with doing anything seemed to be over-compensating and doing too much. They got tired of hiding how they felt. They found their voice. And they shouted it from the rooftops.

Polar bears – if they don't become extinct – often undergo a metamorphosis and become killer bees. It makes sense. Not ecologically, but emotionally.

For confident, well-educated professionals no longer willing to hide who they are and how they feel, it can be freeing – therapeutic even – to get some things off their chest. They want to say it loudly and proudly, possibly for the first time, and not care who knows it.

This is where I first started hearing one common phrase. "I'm brutally honest. And some people can't handle that."

A commonly-held stereotype about passionate people is that they are invasive. They want to upset the status quo and reinstate their own queen bee, so to speak. That frightens people – someone who chooses to be fully self-expressed, sometimes at any cost. Such people feel proud of their stance, but still angry that no one will listen. And if they're not careful, they could be targeted for invasive species removal by the locals.

Brandon was a high school science teacher who ferociously studied social and environmental issues. He was able to inject critical ideas into his subjects at school that engaged students. But he was constantly angry at the stupidity he saw on social media. It was almost impossible for him not to comment on something he felt was misleading or just wrong. However, he would end up frustrated and in long arguments that went nowhere. In a few cases, he had caused a rift between other passionate change agents whom he thought needed his help. They took his unrequested advice as condescending and diminishing of their own hard work.

Claire was a talented writer in her fifties. She hated it when people were wishy-washy, and she felt it was important to be blunt and to the point. The articles she wrote were hard-hitting and got into some heavy topics. They were, however, not being picked up by the magazines and papers as readily as she had hoped. When she put them online via a blog, she was even more upset by the divisive feedback in the comments section. She just couldn't win. Her research and opinions felt critically important, and she wanted to be able to share them without having a meltdown herself or blocking people out.

Gary was an engineer and founded his own light-emitting diode company. His passion was to get businesses off fossil fuels. He saw LED lighting and solar photovoltaics as a sure path to a carbon-free future. Unfortunately, as a visionary, he refused to talk about his passion in any other way except the buzzwords he cared about. And, if a company only dipping their toe in the water got nervous about his aggressive stance on the use of his systems, he got defensive and pushed back. He would lose sight of how he could help them by saving them money today. He let his anger take over, questioning their commitment to a sustainable planet. And he was surprised by the lack of call-backs.

These are just a sampling that represents the majority of the stories I continue to hear today. You probably have heard similar.

## Invasive Emotions

Speaking out in defense of injustice is necessary. And the killer bee strategy can be highly effective in certain instances; namely, forcing a specific party to start or stop a particular behavior through shame, guilt, or sheer numbers. But like the bees, a campaign like this needs a clear target and a large swarm to be successful.

Anger and pride are slightly less difficult than fear and sadness. They make us feel a bit stronger. Ideally, we should find healthy ways to express those emotions, too, at appropriate times and we'd be the better for it. It becomes problematic when anger and fear also become a way of life. Regardless of circumstances, we can feel angry about everything. When we are just angry in general, our source of comfort becomes the consolation prize of pride. We feel proud that at least we "get it" – even if no one else seems to. Being angry and proud all of the time, instead of occasionally, is also a recipe for frustration, overwhelm, and burnout.

In treatment and therapy circles, it is now widely agreed that difficult emotions need healthy expression – not suppression. And that is true. Unfortunately, it's not always understood that healthy expression is not the same thing as dumping on others or treating your emotions as if they are the truth. When this confusion exists, we often see very immediate and divisive results based on our moment-to-moment emotional reactions. Without some time to process or a safe place to share (being vulnerable), those results are rarely productive or provide the desired results had we been given a choice.

---

### Practical Exercises

Spend five minutes each sharing the answers to the following questions (with another human being you know and trust):
- Where today do you feel angry or proud, and are invasively sharing your passion?
- Are you ever upset by the results even though you've shared your true thoughts and feelings?
- Have you ever been so proud that you couldn't apologize even though maybe you should?

---

### The Killer Bee – Part 2

Earlier I shared that killer bees are an invasive species. What I didn't share was that they are the result of human error. An accidental release of 26 swarms cross-bred between European and African honey bees. The hope was that Africanized bees could produce more honey and thrive in tropical locations. So it's really not their fault.

That's what they were created for, and they are incredibly successful by most standards.

Killer bee swarms have some characteristics we often associate with healthy communities. They have a strong sense of place. They are loyal and protective of their home. They take action and will defend themselves, if necessary. That's probably why their expansion from South to Central and Northern America was one of the most rapid in history, despite going largely unassisted by humans.

Killer bees might not be the most loved species, but they have something to teach us. They have mastered the ability to grow, enter into unfamiliar territory, and thrive.

### Critical Mass versus Invasive

More push back came from this metaphor as well. I was sharing it over lunch with the manager of communications for an environmental lobby group, and this was his reply.

"Our action alert system is built on the killer bee approach! Angry people take action. Once, I sent an email campaign to our large list of followers with good news about an initiative. Both my boss and I heard about it from multiple people. They were upset that we would announce positive news, when there was so much bad stuff still happening. They thought people would become complacent and stop writing letters and advocating."

For him, managing an action alert system required making people feel urgency – and yes, anger – because the desired result is clicking the "Act Now" button. There was a mix of professional obligation and personal feelings that we all have to deal with at some point, because anger is a valid emotion that compels us to stand up for what we believe is right.

I hope you never believe that I just think any time you get angry or defend a position that you are doing something wrong – or being ineffective. The key to leveraging your emotions, avoiding burnout, and eliminating stress is being able to answer this question honestly:

Are you angry as a default, or are you choosing to be part of an effective swarm?

When I was in undergrad, it felt like I had a bone to pick with the world. I was constantly focused on finding and fixing problems – even if they weren't there. I rarely stuck with one group because I would inevitably find something wrong with them or their approach.

When the manager of communications rallied his constituent base of several thousand people, he wasn't angry as a default. It was for a valid concern.

Environmental rules and regulations protecting our health, our soil, our water, and our air do come under attack or need to evolve over time to keep pace with growing pressures. Pretending that nothing is wrong will not move a large group of citizens to take action.

But I cautioned him to be very careful not to play with his membership's emotions too freely. A passionate swarm can quickly turn on you if you violate the trust that is the foundation of their loyalty.

Feeling compelled to be invasive is anger-as-a-default. Pride gets in the way of your success, and you risk finding yourself a lone warrior in a losing fight. Achieving critical mass can be sparked by momentary anger, but it is a fire that requires the fuel of leadership, vision, and group buy-in.

For instance, the majority of campaigns against large corporations and governments were effective killer bee swarms. Think Nike sweatshops in the '90s, the Sea Shepherds taking on Japanese whaling fleets on prime time television, or the recent Blackfish documentary played on CNN calling out SeaWorld. Some things are best changed with thousands of demanding customers or voters, and lots of media coverage. Or really well-planned community organizing at the local level.

In the age of information, new tools and technology are being introduced constantly that make this type of organization and achievement of critical mass even easier. Sites that host videos, petitions, and crowdfunding campaigns (all with built-in social media integration) are changing the landscape of what is possible at all scales of change.

Spend time researching tools like Kickstarter, IndieGoGo, ThunderClap, Change.org, and VolunteerLocal. Better yet, build your own technological solutions. Chapter 8 has tons of great info on influencing groups.

---

**Practical Exercises**

Spend five minutes each sharing the answers to the following questions (with another human being you know and trust):
- What is one area in life where you are already part of a highly-effective group cause?
- In what other areas do you see that you come on too strongly or you're all alone, and could leverage your emotions for more success?
- Do you have causes in your life that you can organize more strategically? What are they? How do you feel about them today?

## Additional Resources

- **The Dance of Anger** (book) by Harriet Lerner
- **Beyond Anger** (book) by Thomas Harbin
- **Don't Bite the Hook** (audio CD) by Pema Chodron
- **The Advanced Course** (weekend workshop) by Landmark Education
- **Yoga** (in general) – It takes strength, focus, and flexibility to harness anger and pride for good. I've found a regular yoga practice to be very healing, as well as increasing my effectiveness. And I notice when I fall off my practice.

## CHAPTER 3
## KEYSTONE

*"Courage is what it takes to stand up and speak; courage is also what it takes to sit down and listen."*
~ Winston Churchill

In 2006, I came full-circle back to business and ended up earning an MBA. It definitely isn't what you would imagine.

Before that, I had taken the Swiss Family Robinson thing a bit far – living and working at programs in Okinawa, northern California, South Korea, the Florida Keys, Hawaii, Germany, Costa Rica, the Galapagos Islands, and Santa Catalina Island. This was in a span of four years. My hiking shoes and backpack were well-worn, and carried the aroma of exotic soils ground into the fabric. My sense of adventure had kept me globe-trotting, but my pride took me back to graduate school – and Iowa.

Frustrated with what I saw as poorly run programs – a product of my own anger and judgmentalism – I was determined to fix things. Also determined to use my business background for good, I started looking at Master's programs. I wanted to earn my MBA, but maintain my social and environmental focus. Moving closer to my family would also be a plus. I was tired of missing weddings, funerals, birthdays, and numerous births of cousins and second cousins.

Maharishi University of Management is the Naropa University of the Midwest. A quirky private college in the middle of Iowa, it was founded by the Transcendental Meditation movement and Maharishi Mahesh Yogi – guru to the Beatles. Ironically, it's not nestled in a hippie place like Boulder, Colorado but the small rural town of Fairfield, Iowa. That happens to be fifteen minutes from my hometown.

I signed up for a 10-month accelerated MBA program – five hours per day, six days per week, with block scheduling of one class per month. It was in an entrepreneurship course that I first read The Next Economy by Paul Hawken. That led me to read his other books: The Ecology of Commerce, followed by Natural Capitalism. Something clicked for me.

I thought, "If business leaders and companies can truly take on sustainability successfully – if industry can change – then we've got a chance." It became my new research project.

Post-graduate at 26, I was back on Catalina working for Ambassadors of the Environment. The best school-year sustainability education program I've ever seen, it was founded by Jean-Michel Cousteau (son of Jacques Cousteau, my scuba hero) and marine biologist Richard Murphy (aka "Murph"). During training, the staff were hanging out in a cabin one night on the beach discussing the state of the world, and I asked Murph what he thought needed to happen.

He expressed his frustrations with the limitations of youth education. "Kids' lives can completely transform with an outdoor environmental program," he said. "But if they go home, and their family isn't on board or shuts them down, it goes nowhere. We need to reach the parents, and schools, and cities, so students can act on this stuff when they get back to reality."

"What about sustainability education for adults?" I asked. "What about programs that target young professionals, families, and employees in the city? Wouldn't that help?"

"Yeah, that's a good idea," he said.

And that was it for me.

Having someone I admired and respected validate my ideas gave me the courage to create something new – not just try to fix something I thought wasn't working.

In 2007, I moved back to Iowa – Des Moines specifically – with the idea of launching a non-profit that plugged working adults into the sustainability movement. I envisioned a networking group that also put on cool events and projects on evenings and weekends instead of offering environmental education to kids. Taking liberties with the name, but also honoring my inspiration, I called it Urban Ambassadors.

It was through founding this organization – courageously creating something new – that I ended up learning to accept where people were in life, so that I could deliver them programming that they were receptive to. In this way, we could impact their lives.

It was also where I met more heroes and mentors: Bob Willard, Ray Anderson, Bill Witherspoon, Simran Sethi, and Hunter Lovins. These people shared my passion, were light-years ahead of me, and helped show me another way – a way to operate more effectively and cause the change I wanted to see in the world. That way took courage and acceptance.

In embracing this new outlook, I was lucky enough to start an organization, host a radio show, get a dream job, coach others, speak at conferences, start teaching an MBA course on sustainability for the University of Iowa, and become a consultant. The big secret was that I started leveraging my emotions, and really listening to people.

I started making my passion for sustainability less about me, and more about the communities that I wanted to change. Which was not – and is not – easy.

I still fail constantly. But it's a lot less stressful and a whole lot more rewarding. So I keep going. And I focus on mastering the skills and tools that help me communicate sustainability in ways in which other people are willing to listen.

That's what it can be like to find balance between the over-correction of fear and anger and the over-correction of sadness and pride. It can feel courageous and accepting. It can also feel peaceful and stress-free.

**Critical Questions**

- What is your earliest memory of following your heart and creating something new?
- How old were you? Where were you?
- What happened? What did you tell yourself about the situation?
- Did you learn something new about yourself and what was possible?
- Did you say "Something's right" or "I am good enough"?

**The Sea Otter – Part 1**

Sea otters (Enhydra lutris) have thick fur that insulates them from the cold waters of the northeastern Pacific Ocean. Capable of living on land, they prefer the sea, where they courageously risk running into predators like sea lions, sharks, and killer whales. Up close, sea otters are not much to look at – with rough, dark fur and strong scent glands – but their relaxed and playful demeanor makes them quite fun to watch. Diurnal, they are often visible during odd hours, usually dusk and dawn. And if you catch a glimpse they may be cleaning themselves – spending a lot of time on little things like grooming their fur and untangling their own knots.

One of their favorite meals is a sea urchin. Urchins munch on the holdfasts of kelp plants (similar to roots) that cling to rocks and keep them from floating away. So, by systematically removing urchins from the sea floor, sea otters protect the kelp forest ecosystems in which they live from collapsing. It is a keystone species, the presence of which makes others stronger and is an indicator of overall community health.

When you think of a sea otter, you might picture two lazy creatures back floating side-by-side, cracking open shells on their tummies. In fact, their use of rocks as tools to help them feed on crustaceans gives them quite a reputation as a mammal-genius. Or maybe you think of Disney's sibling otters: Peanut, Butter, and Jelly?

Either way, what kind of emotional reaction do you feel? I am drawn out of my shell into a more playful and adventurous state – and want to laugh and enjoy myself a bit more. I can be pretty serious. And that's no fun all the time.

I love to use the story of the sea otter when I speak at conferences, because it is a powerful metaphor for what is possible. It pulls people into a sense of playfulness. It gives them a stress-free experience they seldom feel at work on their passions.

Tipping the emotional scales back into balance – somewhere between anger/pride and fear/sadness – is not as logical a next step for people who have found brutal honesty and self-expression so liberating. Anger and defensiveness have real value. And there are things in this world that need protecting. You may start to believe there is no other fuel for meaningful action. So, letting go of anger can initially feel like going back to the days of fear and grief. It can feel like giving up, or selling out, on what you care about.

Courage is directed inward. Doing what you feel called to do. Not out of anger or pride. Not in response or reaction to something else. Just searching deep down for what you feel is important in your own life, and then doing that the best you can in a way that also transforms the world around you. Believing in yourself. Following your passion. Learning your true self and then trusting in it, too.

Acceptance is directed outward. Seeing people and situations for who and what they truly are – no added story. Listening without imposing. Meeting short-term challenges with grace and gratitude because they provide long-term personal growth. Being able to let things go easily when it is called for.

Life is messy. Best to get used to. Welcome it. Celebrate it. And live it to the fullest, while making the biggest contribution you possibly can while you're here.

Moving back to Des Moines was my first real sense that I could become a keystone influencer. It was possible that I could give up being right in exchange for progress. I could swim in uncharted waters with adversaries and be okay. I could fly under the radar and actually get more done.

I could have more fun and reach more people.

I could focus on healing my own issues, so that I could heal issues in the community. And it was possible to trade in pushing a self-selected project onto others for being a good listener. That way I could find problems and systematically identify and launch new projects that provide value to the whole community – supporters and detractors alike.

Fast forward. Clients today largely share one over-arching thing with me. They can't believe how much better it feels to move into this space. They can relax more, play more, and make more of the difference they had always dreamed they could.

A keystone influencer isn't loved by all – definitely not by sea urchins – but they always seem to have community support when some try to paint them as an invasive threat.

Courage and acceptance have a funny way of leading to truth and mastery. Truth is very different from honesty. Honesty is being willing to say how you feel. Truth is being willing to listen to how others feel and work to find a shared reality – to find out what is so. And from what is actually so, you have unlimited opportunities to be a contribution.

Killer bees that can push past anger and pride – past their concern of reverting back to a vulnerable polar bear – undergo another metamorphosis. This time, they become sea otters.

Margaret watched the documentary End of Suburbia and was moved. She put out an invite to several environmental groups and showed another documentary at her home, The Power of Community. From that small group, she launched a book club reading The Transition Handbook and formed Transition Des Moines. Transition Towns are a global movement of citizens focused on solving the issues of climate change and peak oil with local action. That group has provided people and passion to countless initiatives throughout the city over the past five years.

It has also produced new leaders that have gone out and done amazing things on their own.

Diana, a retired pastor, learned in church that one in four children was undernourished in Greater Des Moines. She dedicated her life to letting people know this stunning statistic. She brought high-caliber experts into the city to speak on the issue of hunger, then led a team to create an annual conference bringing together the hunger-fighting and local-food communities. That event has resulted in never-before-seen collaboration and programs to alleviate hunger and expand urban agriculture across the metro. Diana formed a coalition of organizations and individuals committed to ending childhood hunger by 2015. Three years later, her coalition took ownership of the conference and is now funding a documentary to raise awareness across the state.

My friend Sheila spoke to my Monday night MBA class on sustainability last fall. She earned her degree in earth science in 2006, then saw that companies were hiring positions to help them become more sustainable. She didn't get those jobs. Although she understood science, she couldn't translate her skill set into a meaningful business strategy. So she applied to Presidio Graduate School in San Francisco and earned her MBA in Sustainable Business. Then, she went to work for a firm in Chicago. After running her own consulting company in Iowa City for several years, she put her practice on hold for an association position implementing sustainability for an entire industry. She knew she wanted to help businesses make a change, and now she's literally helping thousands of businesses across the United States do just that.

These are a fraction of the stories I have had the pleasure of hearing. My hope is that you have heard similar. I worry because I don't think these stories are the ones that get told.

## Keystone Emotions

Committing to long-term, systematic progress in your community is necessary. And the sea otter strategy is critical for this to be possible. Even if a killer bee strategy is successful initially, the implementation of that strategy is often complex and fraught with opportunities to be derailed or undermined. The doers, the keepers of the promise, need to outnumber the detractors and those who would work behind the scenes to see the effort undone.

Courage and acceptance are not difficult emotions. But they are accessible only by rising above fear and sadness, anger and pride. They don't provide relative strength. Courage and acceptance provide real power. And real power carries a newfound responsibility.

Instead of fueling our actions and promises fighting against something or someone, we have to create something new and give our word that it will happen simply because we believe in it. The risk with anger and pride is that the threat is removed. If so, the action and the promises can disappear just as quickly. The fuel is emptied. The fire is extinguished. Courage and acceptance provide a blank canvas and the fuel comes from within.

Courage and acceptance are not simple. They require self-exploration and inner honesty.

Healing must take place within ourselves. We must accept things that historically have acted as triggers and caused us to react without thinking. Courage can only exist in the face of something opposing it. But courage moves ahead in the face of adversity, while anger and pride attempt to eliminate adversity altogether. Acceptance is seeing and admitting how things really are. Acceptance can move ahead towards a future vision, while anger and pride stay stuck in the past seeking blame and retribution.

---

**Practical Exercises**

Spend five minutes each sharing the answers to the following questions (with another human being you know and trust):
- Where today do you feel courageous or accepting and have experienced a breakthrough in action?
- Are you ever surprised by the results even though you're seemingly not working so hard?
- Have you ever healed an internal wound that freed you up to operate newly in the world?

## The Sea Otter – Part 2

Earlier I shared that sea otters are a keystone species. What I didn't share was that they are also classified as an endangered species. Dropping below a couple of thousand individuals in the early 1900s, their populations have rebounded slightly, yet plateaued in the Aleutian Islands and California. Kelp forests desperately need sea otters. And sea otters desperately need healthy environments in which to reproduce. They need a reprieve from being hunted. And they need to be reintroduced into areas where they are scarce.

This is what I referred to in the Introduction of the book.

If millions of people understand social and environmental issues exist and are important… and according to the research they also believe we should change, why aren't we?

Because these millions of people are not necessarily operating from a place of courage and acceptance. Look around. Observe how many initiatives are driven by fear, sadness, anger, and pride instead. How successful are they?

Yes, we need to master the facts – the data – about our problems. But often we have enough facts and data.

We need leaders who know themselves just as well as they know the causes they champion. That kind of leadership would be shaping, designing and delivering messages, programs, and campaigns with extreme success.

Do you know leaders like that? Are you one of them?

### Positive Thinking versus Keystone

A letter-writing advocate struggled with this metaphor, and asked me the following question: "If I stop getting angry, what if I stop fighting for things that matter? I don't want that. Even if it feels better. I want to fight for what I believe in!"

Amen, again.

Don't stop getting angry. Stop being angry.

Getting angry happens. It will never stop. Process it. Express it in a healthy way, and move on. If you let those moments define you – if you stay angry as a way of life, always reacting – you'll miss out on or severely limit your most amazing opportunities to strengthen your community and transform the world.

Anger and pride both have a way of clouding your judgment. You will take action and deliver communication in ineffective ways. Your best efforts will produce poor results. You will not generate change on the scale that you had hoped.

That does not mean you should just pretend everything is okay all the time.

Don't live in denial that unworkable situations exist in the world and need your attention. Don't witness injustice and do nothing. Don't choose to be happy around the clock, and suppress real emotions when you are bothered by the realities of life.

The positive thinking movement is rooted in the social and psychological world, not the physical world. You can't positively-think your way to a new water, nitrogen, or carbon cycle. You can't positively-think your way into a new realm of physics where human beings magically need less food to survive. And you can't rely on positive thinking alone to help 168 million children out of a life of forced labor.

But you can be courageous in the face of the physical limitations of our one green and blue planet – Spaceship Earth. You can accept how the world works, how people behave, and then take powerful and effective action in the face of those realities. You can shape a future that works for seven billion people and growing.

You do that by listening first. You learn as much about an issue as you can. And you look for what will make a difference – where you can contribute.

If approached with courage and acceptance – not fear, sadness, anger, or pride – taking action can be a self-perpetuating cycle. Powerful action helps you gain confidence and experience, then act again. Every new action is more informed than the last. And every new action has a larger contribution than the last.

---

### Practical Exercises

Spend five minutes each sharing the answers to the following questions (with another human being you know and trust):
- What is one area in life that you are already courageously taking on a cause?
- In what areas do you see that you have accepted the way things are, and are moving forward powerfully to create a new possibility?
- Do you have causes in your life where you can be more courageous? More accepting? What would that look like? And how would you feel if you could have a breakthrough there?

## Additional Resources

- **The Power of Just Doing Stuff** (book) by Rob Hopkins
- **The Sustainability Champion's Guidebook** (book) by Bob Willard
- **The Power of Unreasonable People** (book) by John Elkington
- **Self-Expression & Leadership Program** (coaching program) by Landmark Education
- **Visioning** (in general) – Images of what you do want to see in the world are incredibly powerful, especially if you look at them daily. Positive thinking has its place, and its place is in training your subconscious mind to know exactly what it wants, and to always be looking for opportunities to make it a reality.

CHAPTER 4
## AVOID BURNOUT

*"The best way to have new, good ideas is to stop having the old, bad ones."*
~ Ray Anderson

I'm not suggesting there's anything wrong with you being a polar bear (afraid and sad) or a killer bee (angry and proud). Each experience has its strengths and weaknesses – underlying concerns and emotional drivers. Each has a positive, healthy expression for you that can produce something good in the world. And each has a negative, unhealthy expression that can leave you feeling stuck, frustrated, and ready to quit on your dreams.

I am suggesting that the world needs more sea otters (courageous and accepting) – literally and metaphorically. The world needs you to be able to step into that role, and to be at your best.

If you Know Your Self, the next step is to Know Your Strategy so you won't burn out.

### Three Myths Holding Us Back

There are many limiting beliefs in the world. Some we have about ourselves. Some we have about others. But there are three rampant and popular myths about being a change agent that are wreaking havoc on your ability to cause profound change in the world.

I am going to bust those for you now, so you can move forward powerfully – with courage and acceptance – and not burn out. I hope that it's self-evident to you that all of these statements are, in fact, myths. If they remain a prevalent way of thinking for you, these ideas will do more harm than good to the cause that you believe in.

When I first left California to move back to Iowa – Des Moines – I was working three part-time jobs to support myself and my work in the community. My cousin helped me get a cheap room in a house with her friend, Jessie, a second-grade teacher. We got along well. She was incredibly kind-hearted, and I tried to keep things light with humor.

One Saturday morning, I was watching a documentary when she joined me in the living room with snacks. She asked if it was good, and I made a joke about the narrator and some of the flaws in the position the film was taking.

She sat quietly for a minute, then said, "Adam, I'm curious. Have you ever found something that met your lofty standards?"

I was a little startled. I looked over, and she was smiling. I had to laugh at myself. She was right.

She continued, "Good, you get what I'm saying. I feel like it must get tiring always having something to say about everything. And I know you are passionate about sustainability, so I'm not trying to be rude. It can be a real buzz-kill hanging out with you sometimes. You're funny. But you also insert heavy stuff into conversations that are really unimportant and just for kicks."

When I started blogging two years ago, I started asking my "normal" friends – aka those not in the environmental field – what their number one complaint was about me and other environmentalists. Responses were:

"They can be really high and mighty all the time."

"It's like nothing is ever good enough. I don't even bother trying to please them."

"I get you care about this stuff. It just gets a little over-bearing sometimes."

"You really know how to suck the fun out of things, that's for sure."

## MYTH 1
## If I don't influence every conversation that I'm in, I'm a failure.

It is untrue that, if you hear them talking badly about recycling (for instance), it is your duty to set every human being straight. You may have been led to believe that it's your responsibility to be on guard 100 percent of the time against anyone spreading misinformation – or just a bad attitude. Correcting someone in every conversation, or on Facebook until midnight, is not your job. If you stop, you will not be selling out on what you believe in. You will actually be much more effective and happy in life.

Influencing someone in every conversation is not required from you to move your community forward. It is not required of you to cause change. If you believe that, then you may not be seeing where the levers of change really exist. You may be confused about what makes a difference for people.

If you constantly correct people or argue your point, you are inevitably speaking at people who aren't ready to listen. In doing so, you are actually turning them off. And likely not only that person, but also the people who witness the interaction and see it going poorly. They then get a sense of, "Well, that felt uncomfortable," or "That person was kind of arrogant."

This myth results in perpetual fault-finding, and is fueled in part by the idea that "It's all the little things that add up." If that's true, then every little thing matters. Projecting onto others, you can convince yourself that it's okay to go around being a constant voice for change. And if you aren't doing that in every situation, all the time, you're a terrible person. It can become your sense of identity – a type of ego trap you don't want to fall into. "People need to know me as the recycling person," or "the person who cares about childhood hunger," or "the person who cares about this and that."

When you're a hammer, everything can start to look like a nail. But sometimes you're pounding on things that don't need to be pounded on. You're turning people off. And in a different situation they could be really open to what you have to say.

On the whole, you may spend one day unknowingly turning off fifty people, convincing one person, and thinking, "Wow, I made a difference!" Yes, you did. Your net contribution was negative forty-nine on the influence charts.

I get that can be tough to hear. I know, because I've done it. I've been this person. And I meant well. But you know what they say about the road paved with good intentions.

When people helped me see this was happening, I sort of woke up. I didn't let it keep me down. I knew it was because I cared and simply didn't see the results of my actions. I had thought it was the only way for me to be successful – to make a difference. And I thought that I was frustrated because of other people. But it was my approach that needed to change.

When I started to look around, I saw that I could pick specific conversations that matter the most, and focus there. It was clear that I might lose a battle or two by forgoing some conversations, but still win the war by having the really important ones. I was able to choose where I wanted to make a difference – where I could contribute to someone – today. I might only reach three people with this approach, but I didn't turn off fifty. Neither did I reinforce their thinking: "I don't like those smug environmentalists."

That's a big win.

Playing into or reinforcing someone's stereotype about passionate people slows down their own process. They may have been receptive, curious, and ready to look into the topic. If I come along and get under their skin, I can trigger them in a way that stops both of us – them from moving forward and me from making a difference. In that way, it's a negative sum game.

If I didn't understand the scope of the game, I might have kept up my losing strategy, and still felt good patting myself on the back.

The great news is the need to influence someone in every conversation is exhausting. If you don't have to do it anymore, it frees up your time and energy to focus on things that really matter to you. And when you see that you can make a clear switch, it will stop feeling like every conversation is a chore or a job. You won't have to show up for work every second of every day correcting people. It can be a huge weight off of your shoulders.

You can say to yourself, "Great! Where are the two or three people that I'm going to make a huge difference for today?"

And if you can just help them, they're going to make a huge difference, too.

### Critical Questions

- When was the last time that you got into a debate that frustrated you and did not produce positive results for your cause?
- Was it in person or online?
- What is the worst thing that could have happened if you chose to listen instead?

---

**Practical Exercises**

- Avoid debating, arguing, or correcting someone for one week. Keep a journal of all the times you felt pulled to voice opposition to what someone else says.
- Track who it was, their role in the community, and the reasons you felt so strongly you needed intervene. Also record how you felt holding back.

---

Four years ago, my sister was visiting from Alaska with her new husband and his sister – raised in an evangelical Southern Baptist home in Texas.

One day, as I often do, I tried to avoid religious debate with light-hearted humor and sarcasm. I thought I had handled it well, until my sister emailed me the next day letting me know how upset she was. Especially that I had tried to "sweep it under the rug." My nonchalant response came off very condescending to her.

We exchanged a few messages, but I was overly defensive of my actions. I felt I had done us all a favor by not arguing about religion and ruining a perfectly good family visit.

A whole two months passed. Things hadn't been the same since, and it was driving me crazy.

I finally called her from Minneapolis and said bluntly, "Sis, I'm sorry. I'm scared to talk religion with you. I know you're in love and happy.

I don't want to fight because I'm worried I won't be Christian enough in your eyes, and that you'll disown me or something.

I respect your faith, but I know how I can get. I don't want to do anything to risk losing you. You're my sister. I love you. And I'd rather have you in my life than try to convince you I'm right."

In Kansas City last month, I was lying in the back yard of a friend's house having what we like to call a "horizontal conversation." It's simply staring at the sky next to someone in the grass and talking about life.

I opened up about the stress I was feeling taking on too many projects, and my need to learn to say, "No." She opened up about frustrations and sadness with her brother. He had taken their father's death very hard, and was overweight and suffering from several physical ailments.

As a health nut, she was constantly pushing him to exercise and eat better. But it seemed to be getting her nowhere. She was worried his health problems were killing him. Her pushing wasn't getting through, and she had never felt more distant from him. It was really bothering her.

I asked her a question that I had asked myself several times about people I loved.

"What if you could get your brother back? What if you could have a close relationship like you used to have as kids, where you both talked and shared and laughed? What if you got to be in his life again, and he got to be in yours? But, in order for that to happen, you had to accept that he would never lose the weight or fix his health problems in the way you want him to. Would you make that trade?"

She paused, but only briefly. Then she started to tear up and whispered, "Yes. God, yes. I would choose to have my brother back."

## MYTH 2
### If I can't influence my family and friends, I'm a failure.

Your friends and family are the people you care about most. It is natural to want to be understood by them. But influencing your friends and family to support your cause in a way that hurts your relationship with them is the last thing you want to do. And it is highly ineffective.

You probably don't like multi-level marketing programs where you have to sell stuff to your friends and family. It can be weird and uncomfortable, especially if what you're selling isn't that useful to them. Hanging all of your hopes and feelings of self-worth on changing the people to whom you are closest can feel the same way.

By focusing on changing your family and friends, you are actually putting your cause or your passion between the two of you – in the middle of your intimate relationship.

If you want to live a stress-filled and frustrated life, then by all means have a weird or uncomfortable relationship with your friends and family. Not having any friends or family relationships can produce similar results.

As human beings, our lives are relationship-based, and influence is all about relationships.

If you have a passion, take it out into the community. Go out and do it. That is what you believe in, so take a firm stand. And when you visit your mom and dad – who loved you, raised you in their own special way, made mistakes, and are probably still making mistakes in your eyes – your first priority, before anything else, should be to have an amazing relationship with them. The same goes for your siblings, spouse, kids, main squeeze, friends, and coworkers. You want to have a healthy, civil relationship with these people.

Healthy relationships provide you with happiness and some sense of calm. A serene life provides a foundation from which you can go out and make a difference in the community. If you don't have that, people can tell.

If you have an unhealthy relationship with either parent – or both – that's going to ripple into everything that you do. You will have a particular way you deal with authority. You will have a particular way you deal with intimate relationships. You will raise your kids in a certain way.

Nothing is more important to me than having a healthy relationship with my parents, brother and sister, friends, and the people I work with. Everything is easier when that is what I get to come home to at night. And it's only because I have a healthy, civil relationship with them that they listen to me about social and environmental issues.

I recently was asked the question, "Do I have to have healthy relationships with my friends and family in order to influence change?"

To be an agent of change in any community, perfect relationships are obviously not a prerequisite. Perfection doesn't exist. And chasing perfection is most often the enemy of the good.

But to reach your true potential in what you can create in the world, I would go so far as to say that having dysfunctional family relationships will hold you back significantly. My recommendation is that you work hard to heal – especially with parents, siblings, partners and children. Seek to find forgiveness and acceptance for the past. Live in the present. Keep yourself and your loved ones safe, of course. Don't maintain violent or abusive relationships. But don't allow personal issues to hold you back. Do the personal work. Your community will thank you.

This can be a little hard to hear.

Your relationships are your life. They are you at the end of the day. You are your closest relationships. They will inevitably spill out into the way you relate to everyone, and the world. You can't compartmentalize your life as easily as you think. You think you can. But you're wrong.

This myth is often rooted in your ego-identity.

It can start to feel like, "If people look at me as a change agent, and they see my dad doesn't recycle, or mom supports a cause that I don't believe in, that reflects poorly on me!"

For instance, your goal might be to have public transportation and all kinds of alternative, less-polluting options available in your city. So you start a campaign to support a new car-sharing program. In doing so, you might think "I want my wife to stop driving an SUV so people believe in me and don't question my ability to make this happen." That is an unhealthy place to come from and is not furthering your cause. The only cause it's furthering is your ego identity. But it's hurting your marriage.

To be fair, some people will try to use personal attacks if they don't agree with you or don't want your particular initiative to be successful. But let's be honest. The people who look at your family and friends, then judge you because of it, are not likely to be the leaders or decision-makers in the community that you need to influence anyway. Don't worry about them.

The ego quickly loses sight of your selfless passion to change the world. Remind yourself that you're not influencing people just for the fun of it (although it can be fun). You're not influencing people to become more popular. You're influencing people to adopt new behaviors. You're trying to make more sustainable choices available, grow them over time, and eventually replace behaviors that are unsustainable.

You're not just getting your tally up by saying "I influenced three people today. Check." You have a purpose in the previous paragraph.

Impressing people with what your mom and dad are doing should not be your purpose, cause, or passion.

Put your relationship with them first, not your cause. Only then will you have a relationship in which to be influential. And you'll be happier that you get to keep loved ones in your life.

In reality, they may be open to your advice or help. But when they sense that you're doing it because you're annoyed, that they need to be fixed, or that it reflects poorly on you, they turn off. They hear you saying, "I wish you were more environmentally-conscious like me, so people would see me as a leader, and I could feel more successful."

You're not going to get the response you wanted.

Instead, go make a difference in the community and be a success regardless. They will notice and ask about it, giving you an opportunity to share. Understanding and respect stem from the healthy relationship – not the other way around.

## Critical Questions

- When was the last time that you tried to tell a friend or family member what they should be doing differently?
- Was it in person or online?
- What is the worst thing that could have happened if you chose to ignore their behavior instead?

---

**Practical Exercises**

- Apologize for one week. Think of times when you tried to change someone. Think of the times you put your passion between the two of you. Share that with them. Let them know you see how it impacted your relationship. Let them know that even though you are committed to your passion, your relationship comes first.
- Keep a journal of all your apologies. Track who it was, their role in your life, and the reasons you felt so strongly you needed to intervene. Also record how you felt apologizing.

---

On my last visit to see my parents and brother, we were all sitting at the kitchen table. In the background, the TV flashed something about LeBron James and the NBA. My dad started in about the ridiculously high salaries of professional athletes.

I blurted out, "At least it's clear that they produce results and bring in the cash. Did you see the new study in Forbes showing that the higher a CEO gets paid the worse company stock does over the next three years?"

Cue ten minutes of arguing.

This is still my life.

My dad and I have an on-going debate. Not about the value of business, but whether or not the widening gap of CEO pay is actually good for businesses or just the individuals drawing the large check.

As you can see – despite my best intentions – I occasionally still get triggered and turn the most unrelated incident into an opportunity to argue. It's a curse that never produces positive results.

Facebook is a great place to do research. It never ceases to amaze me how many people post angry, name-calling messages, videos, and articles and then get surprised when it doesn't completely change people's minds. The comment section becomes several pages long, filled with defensive and counter-defensive arguments – more name-calling, desperation, and finally giving up.

One of my favorite Facebook cartoons is an angry little stick-man hunched over a computer desk. Someone out of view says, "Honey, come to bed." To which he replies, "No. Someone on the internet is wrong!" I laugh just thinking about it. And I post it often to remind myself not to get sucked into that trap.

## MYTH 3
## We don't have much time, so I need to be louder and more forceful.

You may feel like you need to be hitting people over the head because time is of the essence. You can decide that you need to be even more annoying than you were in the past. You know – turn it up a notch. It can seem as if the fact that social and environmental issues are becoming worse means that you don't have time for all this nicey-nice garbage.

That is a great recipe for burning out quickly. If it's not working now, and you get louder and more forceful, it will work even slower and worse than before. Logic and psychology both suggest that if time is of the essence – and I personally believe that a lot of things are trending negatively – to make a difference you have to work smarter. You need to do more of the things that will be effective in creating change. You also need to stop doing as many of the ineffective (counterproductive) things as possible.

Simple, yes. Easy, no.

And that is why I am writing this book. Practicing these concepts is critically important. If millions of people can't do both – more of the right things, less of the wrong things – then we will lose.

We literally have to wake ourselves up to this reality, and help wake up every change agent we know. We need to help them see that we need to stop hurting our cause – by turning people off – and to be more strategic about turning people on. That is what success looks like – becoming more persuasive in important areas and not messing things up in other areas. Because it can turn into a negative-sum game.

It's tough work. It's emotional work. You can get anxious and overwhelmed, frustrated and burnt out. Every time a new science report comes out saying global warming is inevitable, it can feel like, "We have to do it now! Change, everybody! Now!"

The great irony is that standing up and yelling, "Change, everybody! Now!" triggers and turns off the very people you need to influence. Not because what you're saying is untrue, but because they obviously are on the fence or opposed to your view already – that's why they haven't changed. It's because the process of change is laid out in our DNA, our psychology, our sociology. You can't change how people change. You have to accept that there's a pre-established process, and then find the courage to use that to your advantage.

Wishing you could make it not so is just that – wishful thinking. It's hoping that because the situation demands speed, people could change immediately, and the world would simply be different overnight. But that's never going to happen.

What doesn't change is that people go through a process to change. And yes, a lot of people have to go through that process.

The answer is not to be louder and more forceful – angry and proud. The answer is to get more passionate people doing only the things that will help move others forward towards change, and stop doing things that push their buttons, annoy them, and actually create new enemies.

You always want to be creating positive change for someone. At least do no harm – the Buddhist way. Or turn the other cheek – the Christian way. That doesn't mean you give up. It means you focus and be more selective in your approach.

This short book is about how to do just that. Focus. Be more selective. Work smarter, not harder. Be more strategic. Leverage your emotions, not be taken over by them. Avoid burnout. Eliminate stress. Influence anyone. Do what works. Stop doing what doesn't work. Read on.

### Critical Questions

- When was the last time that you tried to get louder and more forceful to prove a point?
- Was it in person or online?
- What is the worst thing that could have happened if you chose to ignore their behavior instead?

### Practical Exercises

- Re-evaluate for one week. Consider all the projects that you care about deeply. Are you seeing the results that you believe are necessary? Is the strategy being used resulting in more opposition than support?
- Keep a journal of all your causes. Track the initiative, your role in making a difference, and the reasons those leading chose this particular strategy. Also record how you feel about each initiative's chance of success and the rate at which that will happen.

### Additional Resources

- **Free Tips via Email.** On my website (eco-fluence.com) you can sign up via email to receive a ton of free training, including Turn-Offs & Traps: Top 18 Eco-Influence Mistakes, accompanied by real dialogue you will recognize and a conscious response to each situation.

## PART 2
## ELIMINATE STRESS

*"Insanity is doing the same thing over and over again and expecting different results."*
~ Albert Einstein

You may not know the process that I went through to consider selling, then finally deciding to sell, my car in college. I started taking the bus, hailing cabs, and renting when necessary. But you've made your own changes. You know what it feels like to go from having no interest in an idea, to suddenly being intrigued, and soon find that you're taking action. And you've watched people around you go through a similar process.

You may not have seen the steps I took to quit my highest-paying dream job to-date at 33 to work on a state-wide initiative and focus full-time on consulting, speaking, and coaching. But you've weighed and made tough decisions in your life to align with what is most important to you. And you've watched others transition through difficult choices and changes in their own lives.

It doesn't happen overnight. But if you can learn to see the similarities in how all people change, you will hold a great secret. You will be able to deliver your message to the right people in the right way to get the results you want. In doing so, you'll eliminate the stress associated with applying strategies that are destined to fail, had you only known what was called for at that particular time.

Here's how. Know Your Audience.

This next section will help you understand the three stages of influence people go through – Contempt, Curiosity, and Commitment – and how to read cues from those around you to know which stage they are in.

You will also learn the three strategies that are most effective for moving someone from one stage to the next – Showing, Sharing, and Shaping. Armed with this information, you will never have to turn anyone off again.

Not to say it won't happen. Perfection should never be the goal. Celebrate every time you notice that you've done something to turn someone off. Then, call yourself out. Practice apologizing and taking another approach. Those instances will grow further and further apart, until you find yourself having mastered these stages and strategies.

These stages and strategies have been studied by psychologists, social scientists, marketers, and advertisers for centuries. Whether it's to help people quit smoking and drinking, work out at the gym more regularly, or begin conserving energy at home – the process is a universal template of how human beings make changes.

This knowledge has been used for good, and it has been used to sell cigarettes to children. That is not a reason to avoid learning it. On the contrary, it is a great reason to put this information in your own hands, and the hands of millions like you who truly want to transform their community and build a better future. It's a great reason to help alleviate the stress that millions of passionate people feel from running into obstacles that they could have easily overcome, had they understood this process.

In these next three chapters, I'm going to share real-world, easy-to-use examples that illustrate how to recognize and help others move quickly through these three stages of influence. Your own cause and those you need to influence are really the only ones I want you to care about. Take the time to really reflect and see if you can see your own past attempts to influence others in these chapters.

## CHAPTER 5
## **CONTEMPT**

*"Tart words make no friends: a spoonful of honey will catch more flies than a gallon of vinegar."*
~ Benjamin Franklin

Literally just last night, I stayed up late writing this book until 2:00 AM. My writing coach has me on a strict schedule because I'm a perfectionist. That means I organize, edit, and re-write as I write – which wastes a ton of time when my amazing editor could be using her talents to help me. Anyway, I'm still not cured, so I woke up incredibly tired.

When I wake up tired, I break rule number one: no smartphone before my morning routine. Because it was the weekend, I slumped on the living room couch in a big soft blanket instead, with eyes half-open, and scrolled through Facebook. I shared a couple of videos, made a smart-ass comment, and closed my phone.

Seriously, I coach people on this same stuff…

After my routine, I wanted to spend time writing again and opened my laptop.

Just a quick check of my notifications, and my pride pulled me into a half-hour comment-a-thon. I went back and forth about a 30-second video clip related to GMOs. Whatever. In short, I felt justified – everyone always does – and it took me (no joke) ten minutes to realize the rabbit hole I had gone down.

Eventually, I cut my losses. I apologized to everyone on the thread for being tired and grumpy, told them I loved them, and then left the conversation. I had important things to do.

The one strong opposing view was not in the agriculture industry, the grocery industry, the political debate regarding GMOs – nothing. The only thing I could accomplish was potentially ruining a relationship here in the city in which I live and work.

The first stage of influence, where most people start out, is Contempt. Contempt here is not the same thing as hate or anger. Instead, I want you to think about it like a judge would hold someone in contempt of court. A judge holds someone in contempt who is ignoring or not respecting the authority of the court.

With anything new, people will not immediately respect the idea or trust the source as an authority. They are either actively or passively in Contempt towards the idea – actively, if it flies in the face of something they already believe; passively, if they are simply busy and don't have time for something new.

To humanize this a bit, Contempt should not be seen as a bad thing. It should be seen as a natural reaction to being in Stage 3 – Commitment (which we'll talk about two chapters from now) in another area of their life. Contempt results from not seeing how this new idea fits with their existing Commitment.

For example:

- **Fundamentalist Christians** are often in Contempt towards climate change solutions. They are in Commitment to a belief that the world is only 3,000 years old. They don't put much stock in historical climate change data longer than this time period, and assume it is being used as a smoke-screen for personal, corporate, or government gain. But like them, you can appreciate that you are also skeptical of corruption and spin-marketing used to profit the few.

- **Free market capitalists** are often in Contempt towards penalizing unhealthy foods. They are in Commitment to a belief that individuals should have a choice to eat what they want. They see government taxing some foods as a waste of taxpayer dollars, and perceive too much government intervention as a slippery slope towards socialism. Like them, you can appreciate that you also want more freedom of information and choice for people.

- **Right-wing Republican politicians** are often against solving any social and environmental concerns before short-term economic growth. They are in Commitment to keeping their constituents employed and satisfied come election season. Like them, you can appreciate that you also want your friends and family to find productive work and not struggle financially.

You can do this exercise for anyone in Contempt. Seek to understand. It is a matter of degrees, and the more you can relate to those who disagree with you – focused on your similarities instead of your differences – the faster you will be able to be the change you want to see in the world.

## Critical Question

- What are some of the commitments people or groups have that they use to justify their opposition to your ideas?

## Why This Stage Happens

You spend the majority of your life in Commitment. You grow and learn about things you already care about. You largely ignore things that you don't care about – and people who disagree with you. Be thankful for this fact.

If you were constantly changing your belief system and behaviors all the time, the majority of your life would be stressful and chaotic. Society literally couldn't function. Everything would be in constant flux.

This is one reason why highly creative (changers) and highly organized (status quo) people need each other – even if we drive each other crazy. Creative solutions to problems would never be implemented and systems would never be created to support them without the organized. And old, outdated systems put in place by the organized would never improve and evolve to serve the needs of humanity without the creative.

Too much change is chaos, without the strength of organization. Contempt occurs for this reason.

Even if you are highly creative, you operate by an existing set of values and beliefs – your own world view. Obviously, opposing values and beliefs exist in the world that do not align with your current world view. When you come in contact with those opposing views for the first time, you encounter what Ken Wilber refers to in Sex, Ecology and Spirituality as "differentiation." Clare Graves in The Never Ending Quest calls it "chaos."

An opposing idea becomes defined and apparent for the first time. Most opposing ideas are relatively easy to deal with. You can revisit your Commitment to your current world view and simply dismiss the opposing view – passive Contempt. Active Contempt occurs when it is not easy to dismiss. You may take up opposition to this new idea because it is unsettling.

Sometimes, a piece of information literally threatens your world view. It causes you to question your own values and beliefs. And it will not go away. This is very disturbing and stressful. After all, your world view is the justification for all of your life's choices. Your natural reaction is defense. You want to protect your world view from a dangerous idea. And there are plenty of looters, scammers, and "bad people" out there. There is no shortage of reasons to be cynical.

This is why the entire field of change management exists. Change is difficult, even when it's positive.

## Critical Questions

- Where are you in Stage 1 – Contempt in your own life?
- What commitments do you have that explain being in this stage?

## How This Stage Feels

Feelings in Contempt lead you to label the threatening idea as illogical, taken-out-of-context, or a bold-faced lie. You will file it away in your memory for future reference. To do so, you must associate it with similar things. Neurologically, that is required to create a lasting memory. You must connect how you feel about this threatening idea with pre-existing ideas you have already labeled as threatening. Your neural synapses just work that way.

This is how our brains function – label and associate. It saves time. If you had to evaluate every threat individually on its own merits, it would waste an incredible amount of brain power. You would have to carve out all new synaptic pathways, which is highly inefficient.

For further efficiency, you will often label the source of the idea a threat. And so the people sharing this dangerous idea become crazy, naïve, spin artists, or just liars. Again, it saves you time.

The unfortunate part about all of this is that neurological patterning is not necessarily the truth.

It is highly efficient. It saves time. It protects you. But it does so by over-simplifying ideas, slapping a label on them, and storing them away with little critical thinking involved.

You throw ideas and people into buckets that you associate with similar ideas and people. For example, you could have a bucket for "radical right-wing Republicans" or "greedy politicians". The instant someone shares an idea that resembles things you've heard before, you know right where to put them.

Feeling of defensiveness, anger, fear, sadness, and frustration prepare you to ignore or argue.

And this is exactly how others feel who are threatened by your social and environmental ideas.

Throwing ideas and people into buckets is easy, necessary, and neurologically just the way things work. You can't examine every opposing idea that comes your way. But it is helpful to be aware of this process if you ever hope to lead significant change efforts.

### Critical Questions

- Can you identify people in Contempt to your passion project and the related feelings they have shared?
- What are they threatened by? Why do they get defensive?

### How to Identify This Stage

You need to practice listening.

Active Contempt is the easiest stage to identify. Observe. Dead giveaways are anger, argument, heated discussions, or uncomfortable confrontations about a simple comment.

In conversation, you may hear them say:

- "That is so stupid…"
- "Don't tell me you're one of those people…"
- "I'm not interested, period."

Their questions about your passion will likely start with "Why?" because they can't understand your reasons for supporting such a cause.

- Why should I care?
- Why would we do that?
- Why did I hire you again?

In meetings, you may notice:

- Social and environmental issues never being mentioned
- Jokes at the expense of politicians you admire, or environmental and social issues you care about
- Ideas for environmental or social programs criticized as being "a waste" of time or money, or referred to only as marketing initiatives

On Facebook, you may see them comment harshly or contradictorily in response to a post about an environmental or social cause.

It is difficult to identify passive Contempt, because some people express it silently. They are so uninterested a particular idea, they just don't respond. They shut down or go quiet in conversation. They may never comment on Facebook, simply blocking you if they see you posting what they see as environmentally and socially radical ideas.

One way to confirm this is to do a little research.

- What groups are they active in?
- What passions do they have?

Likely, you will find them associated with groups who are well-known for being against your particular cause.

### Critical Questions

- Can you identify someone or some group that you have been frustrated with that you now realize is in Stage 1 - Contempt?

### Showing

How do you effectively influence someone when they are in Contempt? You don't.

It is impossible to convince someone of your point of view when they are in Stage 1 – Contempt. They are in defense mode. What you can do is help them move into Stage 2 – Curiosity. Here it will become possible for you to Share with them additional information that will influence them.

The way this transition happens is simple – not easy. This is important, so pay attention and fight your urge to engage in debate.

Your two main goals with someone in Contempt are to: (1) avoid turning them off with an attack, and (2) engage in meaningful conversation.

The most effective strategy to use with someone in Contempt is Showing.

Showing is the act of demonstrating the validity of an idea without causing an argument. Show them a working example. That could be by modeling a desired behavior yourself or by introducing them to others like themselves that have adopted that behavior. It could also be by exposing them to a successful project or concept in another community or business.

Either way, you want to do this in a way that is not a personal attack on that individual or what they believe in.

This approach does several key things. It makes them aware that an issue exists. It also demonstrates that positive solutions exist to solve the issue. Most importantly, it increases their number of constructive, supportive relationships.

In *Becoming a Person of Influence*, John C. Maxwell describes this as "maintaining integrity, while building trust." It is still important for you to be known for, and stand firm in, your social and environmental convictions. Just do so in a way that moves them from Stage 1 to Stage 2.

To have any hope of moving this person into Curiosity, you need to Show them what's possible – without making them wrong for disagreeing with you. You must accept where they are and, instead of arguing, you must find the courage to look for examples to share and relate to them on a personal level. You need both to make a connection and show them something new.

Ironically, it's often the passionate ones that cut ties with our non-passionate or disagreeable friends because of a difference of opinion.

You need to stay in the game, utilizing these tools and techniques, for it to pay off in the long run.

In Contempt, you need to be Showing.

Think of it like this. You could argue with someone who believes the earth is the center of the galaxy. You could roll your eyes and try to make them feel embarrassed for having such outdated views.

You could speak louder and try to scare them into believing what you believe.

You could also invite them over for coffee and have a model of the Milky Way galaxy sitting on the table. They can notice it, poke at it, spin some of the planets around, and think about what they see. If they have a question, or make a snide remark, you can offer the use of your telescope so they can look for themselves. No pressure.

You can't really convince anyone to believe what you believe. You can't hit them over the head with a stick, insult them with name-calling, and expect to be successful. But you can make something available to them and let it speak for itself. They will choose to investigate on their own, if given a thoughtful opportunity.

A model sitting on the table isn't condescending. You can't yell at it. It's just a model. Same with a telescope. They exist to stir thought. If the earth-is-the-center fellow keeps trying to instigate an argument and prove their stance, just ask them if they'd like to borrow a book or a DVD. They may say, "No," but you've offered a resource and also tested to see if they are moving towards Stage 2 – Curiosity, where you would use a new strategy – Sharing.

My best friend, Mike, is a software engineer at Garmin and co-owns Café Gratitude in Kansas City with his wife. Besides being two of the most genuine human beings I know, they build community like it's their job – which at Café Gratitude it is. Mike was helping me with this book idea by interviewing me and recording the audio so it could be transcribed. When we covered this section on Contempt and Showing he chimed in.

"I have a great example. I worked in an environment with six guys in a group conference room setting, and I wanted to recycle. I just put a recycling bin in the room and it said 'Recycling' on it. No one would recycle. Nobody cared about that bin, but I started recycling anyway. Over time, everybody started taking their bottles and putting them in the little blue bin. I think it was because I was so playful about it, and I didn't push at all. Now I can really see it's just a model showing them there's this thing called a recycling bin. I'm walking over, putting it in the bin, and not really anything more. They just kind of got curious over time and it seemed easy."

While you are finding ways to Show this person new behaviors and successful examples, you often need to put your cause on the back burner to your relationship. Avoid argument. Look for common ground. Look for shared values.

If they try to argue, don't take the bait. Give a very personal answer – not statistics or facts. They can't argue with a personal story. It is something that happened. What is there to argue with? Make sure it's true. Remember – maintain integrity, build trust.

- **Animal advocacy** – e.g. "I work for an animal shelter and see hundreds of dogs almost starved to death by irresponsible owners. It is horrible to witness and I'll never forget it."
- **Health and wellness** – e.g. "I have a family member who suffered medically their whole life, and diet completely transformed their health when all else failed. It also healed our family."
- **Climate change** – e.g. "I work with refugee families locally and see firsthand the difficulties they face. The news from low-lying islands and countries around the world suffering intense floods is heart-breaking. I know how difficult it will be for thousands of those people to relocate every year to other areas – including here."

Story-telling is a critical skill. And your story is the one you can tell the best. If you share your own experience first versus telling others what to do, you avoid being labeled as different and crazy. It is hard to get yourself out of that bucket. It's better for you to make a connection and get put into their current world view bucket instead – with an asterisk that notes "has curious environmental views." Show them that you have shared interests and values. This alone can open the door that takes them from Contempt to Curiosity.

Some people don't have the potential to be moved from Contempt to Curiosity. They may have larger existential needs to which they are attending. If their basic survival needs are not being met they can't listen unless they believe what you're offering will help them meet those needs.

For anyone, paying rent and feeding their family comes first. They could be dealing with a loss or a loved one in crisis. You never know what someone's current pool of concern includes.

Getting to know someone – building a relationship – is a sure way to learn if they are in a position to think about doing anything else. If they aren't able to today, you can stay in touch and help them do something new when things change. Or you could help them solve their current dilemma and build an even stronger relationship. Always be of service to the greater good.

### Critical Questions

- When have your past actions with people or groups in Stage 1 – Contempt been hurting your cause rather than helping?
- What could you do differently now that you recognize what approach works best for this stage?

### Practical Exercises

Find someone's 'Gateway Cause.' You know that the gateway drug theory says less-bad drugs or crimes can lead to more dangerous drugs or crimes. I refer to a 'Gateway Cause' as the secret passion someone already cares about in which you can help them be successful. And – this is the important part – in so doing, you can learn a tremendous amount about their character, their values, the language they use to talk about what they value, and the way they like to receive information. Be a Go-Getter and do anything you can to find a cause they support that you can help them with. Put your cause on the back burner to your relationship.

- Avoid argument. Look for common ground. Look for shared values.
- Ask about their family, hobbies, and causes that they support. Where did they grow up? What did their parents do for a living? What was their most memorable outdoor experience as a child?
- Ask around. Notice what they have hung up in their office. Take them to lunch. Get LinkedIn with them and check out their profile. Do a Google search. Something.
- Ask them about their passion. Listen. Ask more questions. Why do they care so much? What kind of difference does it make? Request more information. "How can I learn more?"
- Actually learn something. Listen to their stories. Read up. But look for any way you can help them make the difference they are out to make. Introduce them to a new connection. Make a donation. Share about an event with your network. Something that truly benefits their cause.

### Additional Resources

- **How to Win Friends and Influence People** (book) by Dale Carnegie
- **Don't Sweat the Small Stuff** (book) by Richard Carlson
- **The Go-Getter** (book) by Peter B. Kyne
- **Why and How Do We Engage** (TEDxCibeles Talk) – Search YouTube for this TEDx Talk by Simran Sethi on what we can and need to learn from others who we perceive as different from ourselves. It's powerful stuff!

## CHAPTER 6
## CURIOSITY

*"I think, at a child's birth, if a mother could ask a fairy godmother to endow it with the most useful gift, that gift should be curiosity."*
~ Eleanor Roosevelt

In 2008, our non-profit, Urban Ambassadors, needed a location to hold a membership party (we hated calling them meetings). There was a new co-working office just south of MLK Jr. Parkway downtown, and they were looking to expose more people to the space.

The founder, Dan, was an entrepreneurial software genius, with several companies under his belt. A great guy to talk to, I got the impression he wasn't inviting us to the space for his own social and environmental interest. As we got set up and the evening began, he could only occasionally be seen off in the distance, rearranging work stations and closing up the space.

As the meeting got under way, some heavier conversations about worthwhile projects in the city began to unfold. Questions of who would benefit from certain ideas came up. Socio-economic status and access to fancy hybrid cars or LEED-certified buildings were questioned fairly gruffly. "Is this just a hobby for rich white people, or are we trying to make a dent here?"

The officers continued to bring attention back to one of our fundamental areas of concern – money. It was in our bylaws and values to make sure people were financially-literate and financially-secure.

How could we ask people to take care of their community if they couldn't feed their family?

Dan could be noticed more and more in the background as the night went on. He would be stopped mid-way to the kitchen, holding a box or a computer monitor – listening intently to the debate. One co-working business member, Josh, was in the building that night working late on a faith-based gaming simulation program. He looked up from his screen several times to inject his two cents regarding community gardening in his neighborhood. They had difficulty keeping theft to a minimum.

At the end of the night, as we tore down, Dan came up and thanked me for asking to hold the event at his space.

"This was really interesting," he said. "To be honest, I don't care much for most environmental conversations. It seems like they are so far out there – disconnected from reality. But tonight was different. I really had to stop and think about it. We have some real issues in Des Moines. And if you're not saying we should all just pay more for stuff – if you're looking for a plan that works for people – well, yeah, I guess I'm interested in some of those ideas happening, too. When is your next meeting? You should hold it here again."

Oddly, I think it was one of the best compliments I have ever received.

The second stage of influence, after Contempt, is Curiosity. Once someone is exposed to a working example that causes them to question their current stance – without being turned off or feeling attacked – they have a new willingness (for the first time) to consider learning more about an issue.

Let's be clear. They do not respect it yet. But there is an opening for learning and respect to occur.

There are two distinct focuses of their Curiosity, which need to be clearly distinguished. First, they will be Curious about the topic in general. The issue itself will intrigue them. Later, as they gain more understanding – which will require you to use an appropriate strategy – they will eventually be Curious about what it might look like for them to take action. Personal change will intrigue them.

### Why This Stage Occurs

Curiosity occurs for the following reason. You first begin to entertain the possibility that an opposing view might be able to coexist with your current values and beliefs. Ken Wilber in Sex, Ecology and Spirituality refers to this as "transcendence." Clare Graves in The Never Ending Quest calls it "renewal."

The once-threatening idea, you once defended against, now has you Curious. Could you have been wrong? There is still an incredible amount of stress involved, because now you are open to the chance that your world view may be lacking. It is an unnerving experience. Your guard is still up, looking for the slightest hint that you are being scammed or tricked.

But you have been unable to dismiss a new idea. The most compelling reason for this is that someone you like – someone you trust, someone with similar values and beliefs, someone with integrity – has shared an opposing view with you. They have shared a personal story that you can't refute. They have related to and connected with you on a personal level. And they seem to be, or know, a credible source of information.

In 2009, the Nielson Company report Truth in Advertising showed that the number one group people trusted for information was people they know – personal recommendations. That is why you see a huge move to online reviews and ranking by the public. And a coinciding industry of fake-reviews by paid internet trolls – but that is another story.

This stage is a gift, for all of the reasons mentioned before. Usually you are able to dismiss people with opposing views quickly. It's efficient. It saves time. It protects what you already value.

But this person with this new idea has proven to be fairly sane in your eyes. They have not done anything to turn you off. They are not arguing with you, and passive-aggressively calling you every name in the book.

This is Curious indeed.

Curiosity is the natural result of Contempt running into logic. After all, if you are unable to label and associate an idea into the crazy bucket with confidence, what else can you do? You are in a tough spot.

### Critical Questions

- Where are you in Stage 2 – Curiosity in your own life?
- What perspectives or ideas have you previously been opposed to, yet recently have begun to reconsider for more investigation?

### How This Stage Feels

Feelings of Curiosity lead you to temporarily relax your labels and associations that occurred in Contempt. Now you begin a quiet search for more information to shed light on this new idea.

Curiosity is the next step in protecting the things you hold important in life. You begin to consider the threat as a potential opportunity, but you approach it with extreme caution. You still have a fear of change – of an unknown world view. In some ways, this stage is even more stressful. It can feel vulnerable to go outside of your socially-accepted belief system looking for answers.

Out of caution, you will seek trustworthy sources of new information – sources you like – that share similar values and beliefs, and that you feel have integrity.

This is where using the Showing strategy and 'Gateway Cause' exercise in Stage 1 – Contempt pay off. Even if you first hear of an idea from someone, you may not seek them out for more information. This is especially the case if they did not relate and connect with you personally – if you placed them in the crazy bucket.

They will not get a chance to positively impact your life. You will look elsewhere.

This is how others feel if you never connect with them while trying to persuade. They may be turned off. But they may also just not be turned on (in a completely platonic sense). You haven't taken an interest in them, so why would they go out of their way to take an interest in you?

They are stressed out, too. They just want some answers, and they'd rather get them somewhere they feel comfortable and understood.

### Critical Questions

- Can you identify people in Curiosity to your passion project and the related feelings they have shared?
- What are they still nervous about?
- Why did they shift to asking for more information?

### How to Identify This Stage

You need to continue your practice of listening.

Curiosity is easiest to identify if you've used the proper approach during the Contempt stage. If you've connected with this person or established yourself as a trustworthy authority, they can relate to you. You may stop getting the cold shoulder or being asked, "Why?"

In conversation, you may hear them say:

- "Okay, but what about…"
- "I'm having a hard time understanding…"
- "Who would you recommend reading on this subject…?"

Their questions to you will likely start with "What?" because they are seeking to better understand the subject at hand – and later, how they might do something new.

- "What is it that animal advocates want to see changed?"
- "What are the real benefits of organic foods?"
- "What can anyone do about climate change? It's such a big issue."

In meetings, you may notice:

- Social and environmental issues beginning to be introduced into conversations
- Teams struggling to talk about environmental and social issues because they lack information
- Leaders asking to track more data around sustainability programs because they can't justify the return on investment with current reporting

On Facebook, you may see them comment with more engaging dialogue, asking questions and thanking people for sharing links to research or additional articles.

Sometimes it is difficult to identify those who experience Curiosity silently. They may have placed you in the crazy bucket back in Contempt. In that case, revisit Stage 1 and work to connect and relate to them on a personal level. Look for shared values. Find a 'Gateway Cause.'

If you feel connected with someone, believe they are in Curiosity, and they are still silent… try this. Invite them to lunch or a social event. Do not make it related to your cause. Just check in. See if there is anything you can do for them. Be a proactive resource.

Reciprocity is a powerful force of influence. If, in conversation, they mention a need they have or something they are dealing with, be supportive. Be a good listener. Offer your time, resources, or connections to help them get what they want.

Don't try to fix them or their problems. Just let them know you're there for them, and you're willing to be of service if they need it.

Really want them to win in life. Reinforce to them your role as someone who they can ask for help – someone who can and is willing to be of service. Let them know you care.

If you don't care – ask yourself, "Do I really want to influence this person?"

**Critical Question**

- Can you identify someone or some group that you have been frustrated with, and that you now realize is moving forward but they are just in Stage 2 – Curiosity?

**Sharing**

How do you effectively influence someone when they are in Curiosity? By feeding that curiosity.

Watch carefully, and don't turn them off. You can help them progress into Stage 3 – Commitment if you can fight your urge to adopt them as your new protégé at the first hint of Curiosity.

Your main two goals with someone in Curiosity are to: (1) support their search for information, and (2) reinforce their view of you as a trusted resource.

They are still stressed and uncomfortable. You can easily confuse this initial Curiosity with Commitment and move forward too quickly. If you do, it will overwhelm the person, scaring them back into Contempt.

The most effective strategy to use with someone in Curiosity is Sharing.

Sharing is the act of fulfilling their desire for more information without demanding action. Deliver what they already are looking for – in a way they will receive well. That could be additional introductions to people and organizations that are experts in the field, or people like them who have taken action and been successful. It could also be loaning them a book, inviting them over for a DVD, or sending them a link to some articles and research from sources they will find credible.

Either way, you want to do this in a way that is not felt as a directive or a command. They will research specific actions they could take only after educating themselves more on the issue. Remember, until now they've been in Contempt. You may have a PhD in this area, but they are just dipping their toe in the water.

Consider that they may not even know things that you consider to be the basics.

This approach does several key things. It allows for their feelings of dissonance to grow without being directed at you. It gives them the space to freely consider another side of the argument and potential consequences of their present actions. It also shifts the focus away from you as the finger-waving told-you-so authority. You can continue your role as a supportive friend sharing helpful resources. Let the experts be the experts and take the heat for any contentious back-and-forth debates.

In Becoming a Person of Influence, John C. Maxwell describes this as "nurturing, having faith, listening and understanding."

Supporting relationships are just as important as in Contempt. You can continue to introduce them to inspiring people or working examples. They need inspiration during this stressful time to reinforce that they themselves are not crazy. You can help them see that not only are they solving a problem, but they are creating a new opportunity. An opportunity to do something positive for people, the planet, or their own pocketbook. Help them see that they can replace the feeling of dissonance with a feeling of pride and accomplishment.

As they start to become Curious about actions they can take themselves, they will need some self-appraisal tools. You can encourage them to assess their own situation. Recommend tools, quizzes, audits, or other ways to measure what might happen if they don't act – and what might happen if they do.

At this point, they also need experience. Don't just introduce them to people. You can take them on a tour, or to a workshop. Help set them up with a risk-free trial. Help them touch and feel the idea, so it becomes less foreign and more familiar. If these strategies are not considered, it is unlikely that person will ever reach Stage 3 – Commitment.

Education is important, but it is critical for you not to provide all the answers. Curiosity must be fulfilled on their terms. Your job is to support and encourage their search for more information – not just your cause.

In Curiosity, you need to be Sharing.

Think of it like this. You could invite someone to jump out of a plane the very first time they ask about skydiving. You could sign them up for a discount membership and start making travel plans to the nearest air strip. You could get them a gift card for a nice body harness.

You could also let them know that a friend of yours is a skydiving instructor and invite them to meet over coffee. You could offer to look at pictures and video purchased during your last jump. You could answer questions about your own experience, and you could offer to drive out to the landing site just to watch a few jumpers hit the field next weekend – no pressure.

You can't magically turn Curiosity into Commitment – Stage 3. You can't rush people into action without first learning something about why and what the change will be like for them. But you can deliver the resources they need at the time they need them to fuel their interests. They will choose to soak it in and take the next logical step, if given a chance with little pressure.

In 2010, we headed an effort to launch a group micro-lending program for women in poverty. We needed large banks to be interested in funding the project. Step one was having leaders from a local bank and two social service organizations visit the Grameen America office in Omaha, two hours away. They toured the neighboring program and interviewed the director. They came back excited.

The nearby program was already in Iowa, having expanded to make loans in Council Bluffs, just across the Missouri River. Energized that the project was both possible and seemed to be working well in a similar-sized city in the Midwest, they shared their experience at a screening of the film To Catch a Dollar at Drake University.

Their compelling story helped us get several more banks on board to write a business plan.

Today, the Solidarity Microfinance program is launching in Des Moines. It hired a full-time staff member and will make its first loans to local women this year. The key was not in pushing an agenda, but finding the nearest successful program and taking the right people to see it.

It is possible that someone will need a 'Gateway Cause' before they will be open to your cause. Don't despair. You can't change the fact that they – like you – have a unique personal growth journey. They can't skip stages of influence, and they want to trust those who are influencing them.

Whatever they ask for, make sure to:

- Acknowledge them for being open to new ideas and opposing viewpoints
- Offer credible resources (books, news, etc.) that align with their current values and beliefs
- Introduce them to positive people and experiences that will support their search
- Continue to answer any questions they have with a personal story that is not debatable.

Continue to be a story-teller.

- **Green spaces** – "I played outside as a child growing up in the country. Now, it's difficult to visit home and see childhood tree lines and streams I used to play in bulldozed for a couple of extra rows of corn – dead trees piled high. I want my children to be able to play in nature."
- **Wildlife restoration** – "I love being on the water. When I go canoeing on our rivers, I see tons of garbage being dumped and all the money we are spending on municipal water treatment – it's depressing. I get a little angry."
- **Social inequality** – "I grew up in a struggling rural community. My family was poor and we worked hard just to stay afloat. We needed help from family and government services. We weren't lazy, and we worked hard to make something ourselves. Now that I'm successful, I believe strongly in giving back to those who are in a bad situation. I want to help others lift themselves out of poverty."

Everyone has the potential to be moved from Stage 2 – Curiosity to Stage 3 – Commitment. Any new learning is movement in a positive direction. It will embolden them. They will gain momentum towards future action.

The alternative is to push too hard, too fast. And that will not produce the results you are looking for.

### Critical Questions

- When have your past actions with people or groups in Stage 2 – Curiosity been hurting your cause rather than helping?
- What could you do differently now that you recognize what approach works best for this stage?

**Practical Exercises**

Get good at inviting people to fun social outings. Plan events that have an educational component or expose people to new ideas, but that are not preachy. Make that a secondary part of the activity. Include good music, good food, and good company.

- Take a road trip. Have one of the many stops be a progressive or unique program that is making a difference in another town.
- Invite people over for dinner, a movie, and conversation on the back deck. The film could be a documentary, but it may be more effective to choose a more entertaining option that touches on a topic in the plot.
- Make the same dinner, movie, and conversation invitation. Watch something fun. Make sure one or two of the attendees have an amazing story to share that might inspire others.
- Host a fun event with a band and food on-site at a local organization that is doing amazing work in the community. Give them a chance mid-event to say a few words about their mission.
- Take people out in nature, period. A 2011 University of Kentucky study showed only two common denominators that environmentalists share: (1) time spent in semi-wild spaces, and (2) an adult role model who demonstrates love and respect for nature. Be that for each other.

**Additional Resources**

- **Three Deep Breaths** (book) by Thomas Crum
- **Zugunruhe** (book) by Jason McLennan
- **Eco Mind** (book) by Frances Moore Lappé
- **CruxCatalyst.com** (blog) by Sharon Ede – Sharon offers a wealth of knowledge and research on how to engage with those who share different perspectives.

## CHAPTER 7
## COMMITMENT

*"It takes a passionate commitment to really thoroughly understand something, chew it up, not just quickly swallow it."*
~ Steve Jobs

In 2012, our non-profit board shifted its approach towards what we called "seed projects."

Seed projects referred to launching new initiatives in Des Moines that fit into one or more of our focus areas – financial security, volunteerism, local food, zero waste, alternative transportation, green buildings, and renewable energy. We called them seeds because they needed to be replicable. That word replicable was used loosely to mean it would have a ripple effect out into the community.

For a large-scale photo shoot, the replicability of the project was that we shared the professional photos for free. That meant dozens of partner organizations were able to use them in high-impact marketing campaigns for years to come.

For a garden at the alternative high school, the replicability of the project was that we documented the process and made a presentation. The lead teacher on the project was asked to speak all over the city and in several other cities, teaching other schools how to engage high school students and overcome key issues all school gardens face.

The point is they are "seed projects" because they grow beyond our involvement – long after we're gone.

The previous four years it had really felt like our board and a few key members were driving the ship. We intended to be a membership-driven organization. We wanted to empower people. But it felt like we had positioned ourselves as the decision-makers, and members were content to help on projects that we suggested. Less engagement. We were giving opportunities to follow, not to lead.

We decided to shake things up.

There was an end-of-year party where people wrote all their ideas on giant pieces of paper, organized into our seven focus areas. We collected additional ideas via email and Facebook. Next, we pushed all the ideas back out in the form of online polls that the community voted on.

At the kick-off-the-year party, we showcased the highest vote-getting ideas. Then we let everyone self-select onto a seed project team. Each team would work all year to launch their respective idea in the city. There were four teams. Each chose a project champion (or co-champions), and I became their coach for the year.

By year's end our performance was as follows:

- **Urban Garden Tour**: Amazing. Co-champions launched three successful tours on three different dates and built great relationships.
- **Car-Sharing Program**: Good. Researched programs and connected Zip Car with Drake University, who is still in talks to sponsor a local program.
- **Native Landscaping**: Okay. The team made it through design and hasn't pulled the trigger yet because there are some concerns about the site being on a private property.
- **Art Exhibit in Vacant Spaces**: Nothing. The champion got busy with graduate school and disappeared the first week.

I thought coaching would be easy. I've launched all kinds of projects. How hard could it be, right? Right.

All kinds of things came up. Not only is taking action hard for anyone, but leading a team to take action in the community is an entirely different set of frustrations. And I thought I could coach four teams at once to do it all.

The success rate wasn't terrible. For four years we had taken on four or five projects, and inevitably one of them wouldn't pan out.

The real frustration was from not foreseeing each champion would be in a different stage of influence themselves. They each had a different skill set. And each seed project was unique in its own way.

Our group coaching sessions could never provide each person exactly what they needed at the right time. It was a one-size-fits-all strategy – which almost never works.

The third stage of influence, after Curiosity, is Commitment. When people are given an opportunity to learn about an issue from sources they trust – and learn what it might look like for them to take new action – they have a new willingness to risk a change themselves.

Again, let's be clear. They are not die-hard choir members suddenly. But there is an opening for action and first-hand experience.

## Why This Stage Occurs

Commitment occurs for the following reason. You complete an acceptable amount of personal research related to your Curiosity. You find your once-opposing view is able to coexist with your current values and beliefs, with minimal change. Ken Wilber in Sex, Ecology and Spirituality refers to this as "integration." Clare Graves in The Never Ending Quest calls it "new stability."

Credible sources provide you with enough new information that you are able to re-organize your values and beliefs to allow room for this idea. It was critical that you were able to re-label and re-associate things, so your existing world view still makes sense – only slightly adjusted and expanded to include room for this additional idea.

Your world view has actually expanded to include more ideas than it was once capable of doing. This inclusion is a sign of maturity and growth from which you can see more truth than before. This happens out of necessity to resolve the conflict and confusion that you were experiencing in Contempt and Curiosity.

Consider the stress you feel related to learning more about subjects you already enjoy – increasing your breadth of understanding. Now consider the stress you feel related to arguing with someone you disagree with about religion, moral issues, social and environmental concerns – your depth of understanding.

The depth tends to be more unpleasant at first. Hopefully, you can see that this is because the potential for change in your life is more significant. Learning more facts about an issue (breadth) is less stressful than seeing an issue from a different world view (depth).

Commitment is the natural result of Curiosity running into compelling evidence. After all, the reason you were seeking new information was so you could resolve opposing ideas. You were experiencing stress. You wanted it resolved. Your original Commitment to another idea was "threatened" into Contempt. You were seeking to return to the steady and grounded stage of Commitment – this time, via Curiosity.

## Critical Questions

- Where are you in Stage 3 – Commitment in your own life?
- What perspectives or ideas have you previously been opposed to, yet progressed through Contempt and Curiosity to take action you didn't foresee in the past?

## How This Stage Feels

Commitment is the next logical step in protecting the things in life you hold important. You realized the potential threat was an opportunity for growth. You overcame your fear of change – your fear of an opposing world view – with the courage to learn and grow.

For instance, you may have been pro-nuclear energy because of reduced greenhouse emissions. You then re-labeled the issue as also being about hazardous waste and human health. Your world view expanded, so now it made sense to consider the anti-nuclear stance on different grounds.

You may have disliked PETA supporters, believing them to care more about animals than humans. Then a friend whom you respect and work with on human social issues turned out to be an animal advocate. You heard them share a balanced view – caring about people and animals alike. So you realized it was not a choice between the two. Now it made sense not to automatically treat the issue as being either-or. Maybe there was a middle-ground.

There are four levels of Commitment of which you should be aware. You will notice yourself and others progress through these four levels as they try new behaviors: (1) initial excitement, (2) tempered realism, (3) individual commitment, and (4) community commitment.

1. **Initial excitement** is when you first hear about an idea, weigh the pros and cons, and become eager to try it out. It all looked good on paper. The stories you heard were inspiring. Working examples reinforced your belief that it would work. So, you jump in head first. You tell everyone.

2. **Tempered realism** is when you actually try the new behavior. Feelings of insecurity creep in from being a beginner, not knowing or not being perfect. Things go more slowly than you had hoped. It may cost more than you estimated. You make a few mistakes. You learn valuable lessons. And it can be a difficult experience without supporting relationships to mentor you through these struggles.

3. **Individual commitment** is when you experience tempered realism and push through to an actual long-term commitment. You endure the struggles of new habits and lifestyle choices. You decide what you can realistically stick with. Often these are very personal, individualized goals that prove beneficial to your pocketbook or quality of life. Due to this fact, you have an extra incentive not to quit, because you've gotten a taste of what is possible and you don't want to go back.

4. **Community commitment** is when the behaviors that benefitted you individually become habits, and there is little to no stress involved with maintaining them. With this new sense of normal – when new things become habits – there is a huge reduction in the mental and physical energy required. That new energy and wisdom of experience is freed up, and there is a big opportunity to invest your time and money into issues that impact your larger community.

Returning to Commitment, you can eventually experience a huge relief – physically, mentally, and emotionally. Both Contempt and Curiosity are high stress. Be happy to spend most of life growing in areas you enjoy – Commitment. Mastering an existing viewpoint and then acquiring new skills and information is fairly straightforward – you just fill up your existing world view.

If you were constantly growing in depth – expanding world views – Contempt and Curiosity would be your life. It would be all stress, chaos, and change. You would never get to master anything.

### Critical Questions

- Can you identify people in Commitment to your passion project and the related feelings they have shared?
- Which of the four levels are they in today?
- Why did they shift to taking action?

### How to Identify This Stage

Continue to listen. You may be sensing a theme.

Commitment is easiest to identify if you've used the proper approach during the Curiosity stage. If you've been supportive and encouraging of their search for knowledge, provided credible sources of new information, and shared meaningful personal stories, then you will likely notice a change in them. Sharing will have paid off.

In conversation, you may hear them say:

- "I didn't realize that…"
- "After she shared her story, I now understand…"
- "Thanks for the book… it does a great job of explaining…"

Their questions to you will likely start with "How?" because their search resulted in a more integrated and expanded world view. They are now seeking expression for their new Commitment.

- "How do I go about adopting rescued pets?"

- "How do I find local gardens in the city?"
- "How do I get a free home energy audit?"

In meetings, you may notice:

- Social and environmental issues being volunteered for as leadership opportunities
- Teams forming to take action on new data around environmental and social issues
- Leaders asking for additional budget allocations for sustainability programs based on ROI calculations and reporting

On Facebook, you may see them comment with logical explanations – reasons – for their newfound perspective to their old groups. They might start re-posting information they learned in Curiosity that tipped the scales for them. If they didn't realize these things were true before, they assume others didn't either.

Sometimes it is difficult to identify those who experience Commitment silently. If they placed you in the crazy bucket back in Contempt, they likely did not include you in their Curiosity stage. Revisit Stage 1 and work to connect and relate to them on a more personal level.

If you feel connected, have been a supporting resource, and believe they are in Commitment, but they seem silent – try this. Schedule time to catch up over coffee and conversation. Don't make it about you. Ask them what they've been up to. Mention an upcoming event related to their Curiosity. Ask if they are going.

This shows that you were listening during their Curiosity phase. It also is telling if they feel comfortable spending time with and meeting new advocates for that cause. They will if they are in Commitment.

Commitment and consistency are powerful forces of influence. If they are willing to attend an event with other advocates, then they are likely in Commitment. You should be safe to ask if they need any additional resources they may find interesting and useful. Don't offer anything unsolicited – you could come off pushy. You can also invite them personally to attend related events with you in the future, with no pressure.

**Critical Questions**

- Can you identify someone or some group that you have been frustrated with in the past, and that you now realize has progressed to Stage 3 – Commitment?
- What made the difference?

## Shaping

How do you effectively support a person when they are in Commitment? Help them stay there, that's how.

This is important, so be clear your work is not done. Resist recruiting them to lead your cause at the first sign of Commitment. You can help them stay strong through initial excitement and persevere past tempered realism, if you understand the four levels of Commitment and how to approach this stage.

Your two main goals with someone in Commitment are to: (1) remove barriers to their success, and (2) build positive support systems.

They are now less stressed. You could easily let them stumble, or turn them off, if you don't continue to speak to their interests. You may leave them too soon, when they need your help the most. You may also push them back to Contempt, or forward but without you.

The effective strategy for Commitment is Shaping.

Shaping is the act of foreseeing and helping them handle possible obstacles without biting off more than they can chew. Go ahead. Clear the path down which you have led them, so they will not regret that they followed you. That could look like additional introductions to experienced individuals and groups that specialize in coaching, training or mentoring beginners. If you are skilled in this area, you might be the right mentor. But if not, be content with others filling this role. You can always be a friendly ear and an encouraging voice along the way. Those qualifications are just as valuable.

Either way, you want to do this in a manner that is not felt as pushy or anxious. They will only take actions that they are ready for and at which they are confident they can be successful. Remember, until now, they've been in Curiosity. You may have been taking action for years, and it's hard to remember what it was like to be a beginner. Try. Be a helpful guide, not an overbearing drill sergeant.

Don't do everything at once. Go for small wins. Remind them of the risks they are avoiding, the opportunities they are taking advantage of, and the positive recognition they can expect for their decision to act. Document the difficulties along the way. Once change has taken place, you can help them re-structure their environment to support the new way of doing things, and make future change easier.

This approach does several key things. It helps remove common barriers that others have already identified and solved via trial-and-error. It gives them trouble-shooting partners in areas that are sure to present problems. It helps them consolidate what they've learned over time. It gives reinforcement and inspiration at the right times.

In Becoming a Person of Influence, John C. Maxwell describes this as "enlarging, navigating for, connecting, and empowering."

Empowering is to lift someone up in an area they feel is important. Remember, this could still be their 'Gateway Cause.' For them to be open to your cause, you may need to translate it for them – into the language of their existing values and beliefs.

It's not impossible to work through all three Stages of Influence in a single book or workshop. Someone you know could move from Contempt to Curiosity to Commitment in a week – or a month. What's important is that going through those stages with someone you care about is a foolproof way to learn what values and beliefs make up their world view.

I'll talk a lot more about values and framing issues powerfully with language in Part 3 – Influence Anyone.

Just know that you shouldn't celebrate success too soon. Don't leave the person alone to fend for themselves at the first sign of buy-in. Be careful not to abandon someone once they reach Commitment. This is where they need you most. It is also the most fun part of the process – the implementation phase.

In Commitment, you need to be Shaping.

Think of it like this. You could spend a year convincing a friend to visit your favorite European city, and then split up the first day when your flight arrives. You could hand them a map with a highlighted route and then go hang out with your old friends instead. You could let them know there is a great audio tour – but they have to ask around.

You could also hang out with them. You could play tour guide in the areas you remember – and take the same tours a second time, side-by-side with them. You could rediscover the city anew with a fresh set of eyes. You could let the look on their face remind you of how it was when you first encountered the same relics. You could make their trip amazing by participating in it.

You can't sub in for someone in life. You can't learn for them – by proxy. But you can make it easier by preparing them for what is to come, and supporting them through the inevitable twists and turns along the journey. They will walk the road themselves if you make sure they have a map and some helpful guidance along the way – whether that is you or someone more experienced.

For the past four months, I've been helping conduct a feasibility study for a sustainable business association in Iowa.

I sit on a Sustainability Committee at the Greater Des Moines Partnership that offers free tools and gives Environmental Impact Awards each year. I also organized an ad-hoc sustainability professional peer-sharing group at Drake University. Five full-time counterparts in varied industries shared non-proprietary best practices regularly – and four more attended when they could. When we learned that other cities were trying the same thing, it seemed more valuable to research the possibility of a state-wide network.

Even businesses that have a Commitment to environmental and social performance need Shaping. And the best mentors – the quickest removal of commonly perceived barriers – come from other Iowa businesses. They are trying to operate in the same region, under the same regulations, and dealing with the same realities of running a business successfully in the post-2008 economic landscape. Presentations by these champions are sure to be framed in language that others can understand.

After interviewing thirty-seven companies about their practices and needs, businesses are stepping up to form a board of directors and launch membership for 2015. The focus is simple. Learn from others what is working and what isn't working. Create friendly competition. Solve larger issues through collaborative partnerships. Build a state-wide forum where it is safe to ask for help from peers to overcome barriers to implementation.

You can help them speed up the influence process by removing barriers and facilitating movement through the three stages: Contempt, Curiosity, and Commitment. Do this by giving them what they need next to make progress, not what you wish they wanted. Help them get peer-helpers, mentors, and other helpful relationships. And give them 100% of the credit for their success.

Continue to provide personal stories. Success stories that resonate with their experience are crucial:

- **Public transportation** – "It took me a while to learn how to ride the bus. Five years ago, the maps and schedules were almost impossible to read. After a few months of figuring out my route to work, and a couple alternatives if I made a mistake, it started to feel much easier. Reading a book and not getting road rage really helped me start my day off calm and happy. Plus, I save over $300 per month not driving a car."
- **Recycling at work** – "I used to think no one at my company cared, and it would frustrate me. It should save money and it's just the right thing to do. Finally, I realized that the only way to know for sure was to do some research and present it to my boss. Surprisingly, she was happy to hear about the savings I found, and asked the marketing to share my positive story with other employees across departments."
- **Water quality** – "The fact that the agricultural community has not led the way in cleaning up non-point source pollution angered me at first. Instead of solving the root cause, their lobby has focused on buying time by weakening legislation and trying to prevent the testing and sharing of statewide water

quality data. Instead of fight the reality, I decided start my own business that supports water quality groups across the state in measuring and visualizing water quality testing – and connects thousands of individuals with the tools to make a difference."

Everyone in Stage 3 – Commitment can be moved through the four levels. Don't be discouraged when initial excitement is replaced by tempered realism. Individual commitment is right around the corner, followed by community commitment if you stay the course.

Take personal responsibility for those you want to influence in finding success. Be a stand for their life getting better. Be a stand that they can make a big difference in the world.

### Critical Questions

- When have your past actions with people or groups in Stage 3 – Commitment been hurting your cause rather than helping?
- What could you do differently now that you recognize what approach works best for this stage?

### Practical Exercises

Get good at recommending coaching, training, and mentoring resources in your community. Borrow items from the seven areas from our non-profit and start networking with organizations and leaders in your community. That way, whenever you hope to influence someone, you can always share a resource with them and make a difference – even if you are not the expert they are looking for. Be a connector.

- Financial Security – money management training, credit unions, micro-lending programs, Junior Achievement
- Community Service – watershed associations, river clean-ups, wildlife restoration, native plant restoration, invasive species removal
- Local Food – CSAs, local farmers, farmers' markets, Buy Fresh Buy Local, Master Gardeners
- Zero Waste – recycling vendors, composting classes, Habitat for Humanity ReStore, vintage and consignment stores
- Alternative Transportation – city bus, cycling shops, parks and trails, Uber, RelayRides, car-sharing programs
- Green Building – US Green Building Council state chapter, green building supply company, free energy audits, health and wellness audits
- Renewable Energy – trade associations, local installers, utility company incentive programs

## Additional Resources

- **Sex, Ecology & Spirituality** (book) by Ken Wilber
- **Becoming a Person of Influence** (book) by John C. Maxwell
- **The Never Ending Quest** (book) by Clare Graves
- **Changeology** (book) by John Norcross
- **The Power of Sustainable Thinking** (book) by Bob Doppelt

## PART 3
## INFLUENCE ANYONE

*"The key to successful leadership today is influence, not authority."*
~ Ken Blanchard

You may not know the details of organizing a $160,000 fundraising campaign to launch training and school gardens throughout Greater Des Moines and the United States. But you've taken on your own just-as-meaningful community initiatives. You know what it feels like to juggle opposing ideas and try to find a solution that makes the majority – not everyone – interested in lending their support. And you've watched people you know tackle complex issues in business, in their neighborhoods, and around the world.

You may not believe that one of my favorite people and most caring mentors in sustainable business is a highly-educated conservative Republican – a Creationist who does not believe in human-induced climate change. But you've had to reconcile seeming dualities and paradox in your own life and work, realizing that the ability to do so is a reason for hope, not concern. And you've witnessed others wrestle through confusion to find resolution with the odd and interesting peculiarities this world had to offer them.

It doesn't always look the way you think it should. But if you can learn to see the enormous possibility and opportunities hidden in the challenges of our day, you will hold the secret to finding a new way. When all others want to throw their hands in the air, you will press on. In doing so, you'll find that you can influence anyone – including yourself – and make progress in the world when you start to feel sluggish and stuck in the mud.

Here's how. Overcoming the three myths of influence in Chapter 4 was just the beginning. Know Your Strategy at an even deeper level.

This last section of the book will help you understand how to pick your battles and prioritize your work – with groups and with individuals – when you care deeply about seeing change happen in the world. Your efforts are critically important. Therefore, you should value your time and your energy above all else.

Whenever possible, you should focus your efforts first on groups – organizations, departments, clubs, and populations – with the highest likelihood of support. You can then use that momentum to influence other groups that are slightly less-likely to support your work. That's how you get critical mass. Let life and psychology work in your favor.

Groups are simply collections of individuals. Even if a group is likely to be in your corner, influence happens one mind at a time. You need to know how to choose which groups to focus on, and to know which individuals in that group are the decision-makers. With them, you can frame your approach using what you know about them as unique individuals. The more you treat them that way, the more successful you'll be.

In these last two chapters, I'm going to share real-world, easy-to-use examples that illustrate how to identify and prioritize groups to approach for their support in your cause. I'm also going to share important tips for approaching individuals who have the final say. Your own cause and those you need to influence are really the only ones I want you to care about. Take the time to really reflect and see if you can find your own past attempts to influence in any of these chapters.

## CHAPTER 8
## INFLUENCE GROUPS

*"Time is what we want most, but what we use worst."*
~ William Penn

Now it's time to get to work. The only way you can help create a healthy ecosystem is to understand, first, what ecosystem you are a part of, and second, what constitutes health for that ecosystem.

You would be surprised how easy it is to feel like you've tried everything and that nothing will work. In reality, you might have been working in the wrong areas, talking about the wrong issues, or influencing the wrong people.

To avoid these mistakes and maximize your efforts, we are going to look at how to identify: (1) your own circles of influence, (2) priority groups to focus on, (3) a group's language of concern and measures of success, (4) other initiatives and tools to piggyback on for a competitive advantage, and (5) key decision-makers and influencers in each group.

### Ecological Boundaries

In 2008, Urban Ambassadors' board identified seven key areas that we wanted to focus on supporting and growing in Greater Des Moines: (1) financial security, (2) community service, (3) local food, (4) zero waste, (5) alternative transportation, (6) green building, and (7) renewable energy.

We used those seven areas as a framework to find other great organizations already doing positive work in the city. We used them to map out a website directory that included events and contacts in each area. We used them to solicit ideas from our members by asking, "What is missing in Greater Des Moines in these seven areas?"

Even today, I use the same map to identify key projects I want to see happen here. Sometimes that means I will build a project plan that Proxymity, the consulting firm I work for, can lead from a strategic management position. Sometimes that means I use volunteer time to work on a board or committee to help another organization lead the effort. Sometimes, I share the idea and invest in it financially because I don't have the time or expertise to lead it successfully. Regardless, the map is drawn on a giant whiteboard in my bedroom so I can reference it often.

In my previous role as corporate manager of sustainability, I was the first to fill that position. With only a rough job description to go from, one of my most useful tasks was to draw a map of every department within the company. I pulled out a notebook and drew circles for each department: Real Estate, Construction, Facilities, Marketing, IT, Operations, Finance, and so on.

That map, and the remaining pages of that notebook, got filled up with research over three and a half years. I jotted down a little more every time I attended a meeting with a department or had a lunch with a staff member. It was an invaluable tool that I credit for most of my success before I left.

### Critical Questions

- What circles of influence do you play in? What groups make up those circles?

---

**Practical Exercises**

Map your circles of influence. It is important that you start to understand and visualize what it is you are out to create in life. You need to see where the critical pieces of the puzzle are, and how they are related. This will serve as a starting point for valuable research that you are going to want to do.

- On a blank sheet of paper, draw a small picture of yourself in the center
- Choose the cause that you are most passionate about and committed to
- Around your image, begin drawing a series of circles representing different groups related to your cause or passion. Those groups could be anything: departments within your company, different groups of clients, names of local neighborhoods, non-profits in your city, social circles or clubs, etc.
- Take at least five minutes to draw all of the relevant circles and name them
- Share your map with a fellow community leader and ask for feedback and questions
- Make sure you can explain the map and that they understand and agree with how it is drawn
- Feel free to draw a second or even a third map if you are working on various causes that are not subject to the same circle of influences (for instance, I have a different map for non-profit work in the city than I do for my job).

## Symbiosis

In 2009, we wanted to shut down a couple of blocks in the East Village to recreate a famous photo from Muenster, Germany. It was a series of side-by-side aerial shots of a city street. The scenes each showed the amount of space it took to transport the same number of people by car, bus or bicycle.

To hold a professional photo shoot on a weekend – with the police directing traffic for one bus, dozens of cars, and over one hundred people – was no small task. It also cost money.

Our initial focus was the obvious choice, the local bus system. Des Moines Area Regional Transit (DART) jumped on as a sponsor, offering the use of their hybrid bus. We used their hydraulic lift to get our photographer airborne snapping pictures from the perfect angle.

Other cycling organizations were a great fit. The Bicycle Collective – a non-profit that repairs donated bicycles and resells them to people who don't normally bike – helped us with a donation. They also sent email blasts to their membership for volunteers.

Because we were short on time, we had to start thinking about additional organizations that would support our effort. The City of Des Moines and the Downtown Community Alliance both cared about controlling traffic congestion. They helped by speeding up our permitting process to close down East Locust for two hours. The Neighborhood and Natural Recreation Protection Project (NNRPP) was fighting an extension of Martin Luther King, Jr. Drive north towards Ankeny. The additional traffic would be sent through a historic neighborhood. They sponsored the photo shoot and did outreach for volunteers, as well.

We approached MODUS – a mechanical, electrical, plumbing and technology engineer firm – because they had worked on several large sustainability projects in Iowa and their owners had a passion for community work.

They sponsored and saved us money on traffic barriers and signage. We also reached out to Center on Sustainable Communities (COSC) – a residential green building non-profit. They were not focused on transportation, but had done great work around sustainability for the state, and were a leader in promoting progressive action. The fact that we already had DART, the Bicycle Collective, the Downtown Community Alliance, and NNRPP supporting us, gave us credibility in their eyes.

The event went better than we could have hoped. Over one hundred cyclists participated and it was 103 degrees Fahrenheit that afternoon. Our team had the lead singer of the Nadas – a popular Iowa band – playing acoustic guitar at the Continental pub next door. Everyone celebrated there, and cooled off with drinks after the shoot was over.

When I was hired at my previous job, it was a company-wide job description. My position, however, was placed in the Construction department. LEED-certification for all new buildings, roughly thirty per year, was a big commitment they had made prior to my arrival. Because they didn't know yet how to fulfill that promise, Construction made the most sense. Instead of spreading myself thin across the company, I spent the first year focused on the two departments immediately upstream and downstream from Construction – Real Estate and Facilities. It helped our cause build momentum and support before branching out into the company.

## Critical Questions

- What groups of people can you target first that are most likely to support your cause?
- How can you build momentum and critical mass to bring others on board?

**Practical Exercises**

Prioritize the groups you want to approach. Save yourself time, money, and energy. Ecological communities are only as successful as the species that fill niche roles and benefit others. Without symbiotic relationships, nature would collapse. Strategic partnerships with groups – departments, businesses, non-profits, government agencies, associations, etc. – provide two key benefits. They have money to donate that individuals don't. They also have large lists of membership they can share your project or cause with. Utilize both options.

**Stage 3 – Commitment**
First, make a list of groups that are actively Committed to the mission/vision of your cause or project. It is important to get quick wins and start building a list of supporters.
Second, make a list of groups whose mission/vision aligns with the outcomes of your cause or project. They might not share the same overall mission/vision, but would see this particular result as helping their own. As long as you have a credible list of initial supporters, they will likely join you.

**Stage 2 – Curiosity**
Third, make a list of groups that are Curious about the mission/vision or outcomes of your cause or project. Many in the sustainability movement have chosen a particular specialty – energy, water, waste, social justice, etc. – but still have a passion for the big picture. By the time you approach them, you will have a diverse list of supporters, which will pique their Curiosity and increase the likelihood of them joining.

**Stage 1 – Contempt**
Don't approach these groups unless you absolutely must. Even then, do so only once you've built a diverse coalition of supporters that lend credibility and authority to your cause or project. Involving those in Contempt early will slow and likely derail progress before you can ever gain meaningful momentum or critical mass.

## Fertile Soil

My last mapping exercise using Urban Ambassadors' seven areas was about six months ago. It needs updating, but looks like this:

1. **Financial Security** – group micro-lending for women in poverty, crowdfunding a copy of Dave Ramsey's Financial Peace University for every church/community center in the metro
2. **Community Service** – native/wildlife restoration, water quality site for watershed groups
3. **Local Food** – a garden for every school, increase attendance at Hope for the Hungry conference
4. **Zero Waste** – help spread the word about ReWall, raise awareness about landfill mining
5. **Alternative Transportation** – Zip Car at Drake, Megabus between MSP and KC, Uber app
6. **Green Building** – new conference for efficiency/small homes and affordable housing groups
7. **Renewable Energy** – include in efficiency/small homes/affordable housing conference

These are things I care about in the city. It's always nice to have a list of ideas behind each one that I believe would make a difference. Many of these things have happened, are happening, or have been shared with other leaders in the community in hopes they will happen soon.

That's because I've spent the last six years doing the Practical Exercise from Chapter 7 – Commitment. Go back and review that now, if you have time. By building my network, and spending time learning what each industry is working on in my city, it's easier for me. It's easier for me to know what projects will make a difference, which groups are likely to support those projects, who to approach in those groups, and how to approach them.

At my previous job, Nick was a co-worker in the Real Estate department. He was a very smart guy, and his cousin was a friend who owned his own green building company.

Nick approached me because he was scheduling educational sessions for his department. He knew Construction was doing a lot with LEED-certification, and believed that they weren't leveraging our green building efforts like they should.

All new construction was being LEED-certified (Leadership in Energy & Environmental Design). We had over eighty certified stores and more under construction when I left. Seven were certified at Gold, and thirty-four were certified at Silver. He knew that Real Estate was out searching for sites and didn't know clearly what Construction was working on.

He wasn't sure how to propose learning about it as a valuable use of their time.

I sat with him and asked a simple and important question.

"Can you summarize what Real Estate does in two or three short sentences? In your language, tell me what you are most concerned about getting done in your department?"

Nick knew more than I ever would about the Real Estate department. He worked in it every day. I was a just a tourist. So I needed a crash course from him. I offered a suggestion so he would understand what I was looking for. "It could be 'buying cheap land' or something simple like that."

He countered, "Okay, I see what you mean. In that case, no. We really care about three things: finding good sites, getting sites under contract, and getting sites permitted for build."

I thanked him, "Okay. Knowing that, it's now our job to communicate to Real Estate how green building will help you: find good sites, get sites under contract, and get sites permitted for build. If we can't do that, we can't do much."

The next question I had for Nick was, "How does Real Estate measure success? What metrics tell you if you're doing a good job at finding good sites, getting sites under contract, and getting sites permitted for build?

Think about your weekly meetings or quarterly performance reviews. What numbers are important?"

"Easy," he said, "besides the obvious – number of sites that meet our criteria – what we really talk about are sites-per-market and percentage of our annual pipeline filled for Construction."

The company operates over 400 locations in eleven states. Each market is usually a specific city and can only support a certain number of stores. So, they track progress towards reaching that goal. The Construction department has a goal of building a certain total number of stores per year. They can only do that if Real Estate has a full pipeline of sites under contract and permitted for build.

"Perfect," I said, "We'll make sure we also talk about how green building can help you get sites in certain markets, and help fill your pipeline each year."

**Critical Questions**

- Do you know the language of concern for each group you are trying to influence?
- Do you know how they measure success or quality?

**Practical Exercises**

Begin filling out your map. You have to understand what ideas will grow in each group. Every ecosystem has soil that is fertile, but those nutrients only support certain types of plant life. It's your job to understand the particular soil composition in your community, so you plant seeds that have a chance of taking root. To do that, two things are important to know: (1) a particular group's language of concern, and (2) how they measure success or quality.
- Pick one of your groups/circles that you most want to successfully influence.
- Make sure it matters to you – I want you to put down this book today freed up to take new action.
- What is the language of concern for your group? Try to summarize what they care about in three short sentences or less. Here's a hint: use action words (verbs).
- Consider how they measure quality. How does this group keep score? What numbers matter to them that they keep track of?

### Adaptation

Several strategic things aligned to help our transportation photo shoot find support. DART was re-organizing some of its bus routes. It was in an effort to improve service, but they knew they could never make everyone happy. So, they were looking for ways to market their larger impact in the community. Professional photos that told a story were a perfect fit.

The Downtown Community Alliance was revamping their old website and needed high-quality photography that promoted downtown and marketed their initiatives to reduce traffic congestion. We shot the photos with the state capital in the background, perfectly framed by East Locust mixed-use commercial buildings.

NNRPP was trying to raise awareness about the MLK Jr. Drive extension. COSC was in the midst of strategic planning and considering expanding their scope beyond residential green building to include other community sustainability issues – like transportation.

Some of these we stumbled upon by chance. Others we knew about through our networks and communicated clearly how they would align when we approached each organization.

I asked Nick, "What is happening in real estate? What initiatives do you already have under way? What tools do associates already use to get their job done?"

He ran through a few things in his head. "I don't know. Our only initiative is to get sites and get them yesterday."

But we have just starting talking about how we could do better at communicating the company brand in tough markets."

"What do you mean?" I asked. "How do you do that?"

"Well," he explained, "For example, one real estate representative (RDR) was recently asked for a white paper from a local City Council. Another gave a PowerPoint presentation at a community meeting. Both times, they just came up with it themselves. Marketing didn't have anything ready for them, so it wasn't the best quality."

"Okay, great," I said. "In our presentation, we can also offer to help you build templates for stuff like this, and include sustainability information along with our traditional branding."

### Critical Questions

- In your target groups, what initiatives could you piggyback off?
- What tools or initiatives are already under way that you could align with and borrow from their existing momentum?

**Practical Exercises**

Identify existing efforts that are already under way. Every organism in an ecosystem must learn to adapt over time to survive. Some use camouflage. Some hop a ride on a friendly breeze or a larger animal. You need to become skilled at identifying adaptation strategies that can jump start your own cause or project. This can significantly short-cut the time, money, and energy it takes to reach your intended goal.

- Write down the major campaigns or initiatives that your target group is already committed to. How can your cause enhance or align with those initiatives?
- Write down the major tools and resources that your target group is already using to get their work done. How can information about your cause integrate quickly into those?
- People aren't really afraid of change, as much as they are afraid of too much change – all at once. They don't want to be overwhelmed. People are resilient. But they don't appreciate becoming a dumping ground for every new idea.

## Pollinators

Long before we kicked off the transportation photo shoot in the East Village – "Shoot Your Commute" – we built a team to lead the effort. That team was full of specific types of people: passionate socialites, organized leaders, and key decision-makers.

The passionate socialites spread the word, making it possible to get over one hundred volunteers outside on a 103 degree Fahrenheit afternoon. The also insisted the event be fun, with music, food, and drinks afterward, because they understood what it takes to get people motivated.

The organized leaders created agendas, action items, and assigned tasks to people on the team. They followed up with team members to make sure everything happened on our tight timetable.

The key decision-makers were there to enlighten our team. They shared what it would take to convince their own organizations, as well as others, to join the effort. Decision-makers are also very much in tune with social, economic, and political current events. They have to be. And that wisdom can come in very handy when strategically trying to get a project off the ground.

Nick and I identified what fertile soil looked and sounded like for the Real Estate department, then shifted our attention to the socialites, leaders, and decision-makers in his department. Those were people that our message needed to resonate with.

I asked him, "Who calls the shots in Real Estate? Not just who is in charge, but who gets listened to? And why?"

He thought for a moment. "Well, there's the obvious, our senior vice president. But the real estate development representatives (RDRs) are strong voices. It's their job to be out in the markets working with developers to find sites and get them under contract. They go to our local meetings and are the first face of the company that our communities see and hear from."

"Great," I said. "Write down the names of the four RDRs. It's our job to make the presentation connect with them, as well as the senior vice president. So, we need to know a little more about them."

### Critical Questions

- In your target groups, who will most effectively spread your message?
- Who will be organized enough to implement change?
- Who will make the final decision?

The next chapter is focused on how to influence individuals, so I'm going to skip right to what happened.

I helped Nick prepare and deliver a presentation called "How LEED Can Help Get Sites."

Everything in the presentation tied back to our discussion, and it resonated with all the right people. We were asked to help Real Estate create a new white paper, a PowerPoint presentation, and some large color photo boards they could share with external stakeholders.

These contained great company branding information from the Marketing department –my next target group – as well as green building and company-wide sustainability information.

Serendipity struck, and two months later a golden opportunity dropped in our lap.

Rob, one of the RDRs, came to my desk and said, "Adam, you know that presentation you gave? Can you come with me to Fayetteville and give something similar? The City Council is just like you. They love the earth and are asking all these questions about LEED that I can't answer. I need your help."

Those were his words. I can't make this stuff up. "They love the earth." What could I do? I was sold.

It turned out that we were bidding against a competitor for city property. The Council asked for a closed bid and a company presentation. Our competitor gave a bland company profile. We talked about our philanthropy, our company sustainability initiatives, and our commitment to LEED-certification in all new builds. Our bid was $48,000 lower than the competition. The Council still voted to sell us the property instead.

It was a huge win for sustainability inside our company. The public meeting was video-recorded. We were able to use images and quotes from the decision to tell a much larger story throughout the company about the value of our efforts. And every RDR wanted to study more about LEED and sustainability so they could be better prepared to answer questions in tough markets like Fayetteville.

**Practical Exercises**

Identify the socialites, leaders, and decision-makers in your target groups. Every ecosystem has pollinators that are essential for growth and progress. Ideas and action must spread like pollen for your cause or project to become successful. To facilitate that happening, you need to know those within your target groups who need to be influenced. In the next chapter, you will learn how to best influence these individuals. For now, you need to first identify who they are.

- Write down the name(s) of the most popular, friendly individuals in your target group. Who is liked and fun to be around?
- Write down the name(s) of the most respected voices in your target group. Who is highly competent and listened to by all?
- Write down the names(s) of the final decision-makers in your target group. Who does it ultimately come down to for a commitment or a change?
- If you don't know, you need to utilize your network to learn more about their culture. Ask.

**Huge Short-Cut**

Community-based social marketing (CBSM) is the most rigorous, scientifically-based method that I've ever studied to shorten the length of time it takes to move groups of people to change their behavior. Granted, it requires a period of research and investigation that does not align well with all organizations' programming or funding calendar. But that time is spent uncovering the specific design elements (most represented in the lessons in this book) of a campaign that will have the desired result from the target population. I've seen entire departments train their staff in CBSM and transform their ability to make a difference.

**Additional Resources**

- **Fostering Sustainable Behavior** (book) by Doug McKenzie-Mohr
- **Switch** (book) by Chip Heath
- **The New Sustainability Advantage** (book) by Bob Willard
- **Leading Change Toward Sustainability** (book) by Bob Doppelt
- **Community-Based Social Marketing** (workshops) by Doug McKenzie-Mohr

## CHAPTER 9
## INFLUENCE INDIVIDUALS

*"The most important factor in inspiring pro-environmental behavior is human relationships – the dialogue and discussions between people."*
~ Maggie Melin

You may be trying to influence key socialites, leaders, or decision-makers in a target group. Or you may be trying to share your passion with, and be better understood by, a family member.

Either way, there are dozens of tips for how to connect with and influence individuals – each one of them being unique.

The obvious is to look for cues in their behavior. Determine which stage of influence they are currently in, and utilize *Part 2 – Eliminate Stress* in this book to apply the appropriate strategy for that stage.

If they are in Stage 1 – Contempt, you need to focus on building trust first. Likely, that will be by helping them with their own 'Gateway Cause.' This process will not only build trust, but teach you valuable information about how they like to consume information and from what sources.

As you go about identifying someone's 'Gateway Cause,' it is important to keep your own integrity intact. I'm not encouraging you to sell out on your beliefs. No one said go door-knocking for a candidate you disagree with, or donate to an organization that is destroying sensitive ecosystems. Find something they believe in that you can contribute to in good conscience.

In her TEDxCibeles talk *Why and How Do We Engage?* Simran Sethi tells a story of her friend, Cade. Cade is an ex-military, libertarian hunter who teaches technology. Simran is a left-leaning, Indian American journalist. Her story centers on what Cade does day-to-day, not his beliefs.

She says, "Who is the bigger environmentalist? Cade is far more intimate with the sources of his food than I will ever be. Cade conserves natural resources because it makes good common sense. Cade drives an efficient car, more because it saves money than it saves the planet. And Cade would never call himself and 'environmentalist.' Despite the fact that he can build his own shelter, grow and hunt his own food, that title is reserved for left-leaning hippies like me."

I am asking that you dig deep to find compassion and commonalities with a fellow human being. In order to do that, you may need help in laser-focusing your approach to that individual's unique eco-personality type. This is so you can connect. It is not to lose yourself. Being authentically who you are and finding commonalities with others is the goal here.

## Eco-Personality Types

Jacquelyn Ottman is a renowned green marketing consultant and the author of The New Rules of Green Marketing. In it, she writes about four green interest segments: Resource Conservators, Outdoor Enthusiasts, Health Fanatics, and Animal Lovers.

In her words, "Even the most eco-aware consumers tend to prioritize their environmental concerns. We derived the segmentation from empirical evidence and offer it as a supplement to the Natural Marketing Institute (NMI) segmentation to help you add relevance and precision to efforts targeting the deeper green consumers."

For your clarity, the NMI segmentation itself mirrors the four levels of Stage 3 – Commitment, but related to purchasing patterns.

Initial excitement, tempered realism, individual commitment, and community commitment are instead referred to as drifters, conventionals, naturalites, and LOHAS (Lifestyles of Health and Sustainability).

Notice that Ottman isn't replacing NMI's work, but offering you a helpful supplement – an added bonus. She's saying that the greenest of green consumers have clear priorities. The eco-personality of green fanatics lends them to be one of four unique types: Resource Conservators, Outdoor Enthusiasts, Health Fanatics, and Animal Lovers.

But what about non-fanatics? You aren't necessarily marketing products to willing buyers. You are a change agent in the trenches.

I truly believe, and experience has taught me, that everyone has potential. They are a hero-waiting-to-happen, and if you treat them as such you will be much farther along on your road to stress-free sustainability.

Ottman uses her four green interest segments to talk about "deep green" consumers. But those individuals weren't born that way. They had potential from an early age, and it began to express itself over time as they became aware of social and environmental issues.

You will find much more value in your own passion or cause if you can trace those four segments back to their origin. In this way, Ottman's research (while great for helping businesses sell environmentalists more stuff) becomes more useful for what you actually want — increased ability to influence heroes-waiting-to-happen in your life. You get better at persuading for the planet.

### Type 1 – Health Focused

Health Fanatics start out with a general interest in health. People care about their well-being and vitality from an early age and demonstrate subtle behavioral and verbal hints. Where a fanatic may run marathons, someone with potential likely takes walks, goes to the gym, or eats their vegetables – probably from a big box grocer, but vegetables all the same.

### Type 2 – Happiness Focused

Animal Lovers are sometimes born, and you know it from a young age. And some come to support animal protection later in life. These people tend to empathize easier with other people, and have an interest in social issues. They care for children and try to give a voice to those perceived as under-served. As a first step, they often resonate most with larger animals that more visibly express emotions and attachments – pets, apes, dolphins, elephants, etc. Over time, all people and sentient beings begin to benefit from their inner sense of justice and fairness.

### Type 3 – Resource Focused

Resource Conservators often start out from meager beginnings and are taught the value of thrift. Being raised on a farm makes one resourceful, hoarding things for future use. A need for efficiency and a do-it-yourself attitude are great indicators that someone may be heading in this direction. It's also just good common sense to some people not to waste what they have.

### Type 4 – Recreation Focused

Outdoor Enthusiasts have usually experienced a place they love being threatened by environmental harm. Those with potential likely recreate outdoors, but have limited environmental awareness. They probably ride ATVs, rock climb, hike and camp, or hunt and fish with little thought to preserving their playground. But that usually changes over time.

Are you confused? Here are some helpful hints to clarify:

Your friend is a runner, but on trails. Ask her why. She may tell you how much she loves being outside (recreation) or that this is the only group she could find that paces at her desired heart-rate (health).

Your boss wants to donate to a habitat restoration project. Inquire further. Is it because she feels it's unfair we have destroyed wild animals' homes (happiness) or because she believes in ecosystem services that we humans can't replicate without spending a fortune (resources)?

Asking good questions, and active listening, are your two best friends.

And once you understand someone's eco-personality type, you can more easily identify a 'Gateway Cause' of theirs you can support.

### Critical Questions

- Do you understand the causes and passions of the people you are trying to influence?
- Have you taken the time to get to know them and their interests?

---

**Practical Exercises**

Identify an individual's eco-personality type. Begin to laser-focus your approach. Reference your list of pollinators – key socialites, leaders, and decision-makers – from the previous chapter. Or choose a family member or friend with whom you've grown distant because of eco-arguments in the past.
- What cause and passions do they support?
- What are some of their regular daily habits?
- What are some of their favorite activities?
- Are they Type 1 – Health Focused, Type 2 – Happiness Focused, Type 3 – Resource Focused, or Type 4 – Recreation Focused?
- Once you've identified their likely eco-personality type (or two), look into your heart and find a way to support them in their passion without compromising your own integrity. What would that look like? What could you do today to contribute to their cause?

---

### Values

The key to untangling eco-confusion is first understanding that values are not the same things as behaviors. Values go deeper.

Have you ever met someone you considered an "environmentalist" and been surprised to find they didn't understand a common issue you thought was standard knowledge?

Have you ever been discussing an issue with a fellow social activist and suddenly found yourself in total disagreement on the solution?

You may be shocked to learn that we have all had these experiences. The longer you work on sustainability, the more likely you will come face-to-face with dualities and contradictions. Imagine how easy that makes it to experience miscommunication with a hero-waiting-to-happen. Eco-confusion is all too commonplace. And it can derail your ability to influence if you aren't careful.

It is easy and convenient to blame these frustrating experiences on the other person's ignorance or lack of caring. While at times there is truth to those judgments, that mindset is a weak place to come from. What you need is an approach that gives you insights, and tools to act on them. Values-based listening is that approach.

In *The Environmental Case,* Judith Layzer writes, "Divergent problem definitions – stemming from intractable value conflicts – remain at the heart of all environmental battles."

Think about this list of environmental issues listed in the Introduction to this book. You likely read that list and had two thoughts, shared by most socially- and environmentally-concerned citizens: "That is depressing," and "You forgot to mention [x, y, z]."

Here are some more helpful thoughts to consider. Instead of feeling stuck, they will prime your ability to take action.

"I've been an environmentalist for [x] years, and consider myself somewhat of an expert.

And I'm still not fully informed on all of these topics."

"I'm not taking action in all of these areas to make the difference I could. Realistically, who could tackle all of those problems at once?"

"When I'm in conversation with someone who does not have an environmental studies major, and does not work in social and environmental industries, how do I connect an issue that I'm passion about with something that is important and relevant to them?"

The answer is values.

If you share my personal philosophy that every person is a hero-waiting-to-happen, then it makes sense to go beyond the content of the conversation. You must look for the underlying context instead.

Values are not behaviors. For instance, these lists of value-words for each type of eco-personality shed light on this difference. You need to go deeper than behaviors to find common ground – to build a relationship on common values and work from there.

**Type 1 – Health Focused people** hold values like: feeling good, wellness, strength, and longevity. Related values from other types that will resonate include:
- Type 2 – Happiness Focused: empowerment, ability, and access.
- Type 3 – Resource Focused: responsibility, providing, and sustenance.
- Type 4 – Recreation Focused: vigor and joy.

**Type 2 - Happiness Focused people** hold values like: fairness, justice, equality, and caring. Related values from other types that will resonate include:
- Type 1 – Health Focused: empowerment, ability, access, and providing.
- Type 3 – Resource Focused: responsibility.
- Type 4 – Recreation Focused: joy and access.

**Type 3 – Resource Focused people** hold values like: efficiency, productivity, practicality, and common sense. Related values from other types that will resonate include:
- Type 1 – Health Focused: providing and sustenance.
- Type 2 – Happiness Focused: responsibility.
- Type 4 – Recreation Focused: innovation, discovery, creativity, and invention.

**Type 4 – Recreation Focused people** hold values like: playfulness, competition, freedom, and fun. Related values from other types that will resonate include:
- Type 1 – Health Focused: vigor and joy.
- Type 2 – Happiness Focused: empowerment, ability, and access.
- Type 3 – Resource Focused: innovation, discovery, creativity, and invention.

Values are the reason why someone who believes in social justice and resource use (fairness for others) can butt heads with someone who only believes in resource efficiency (self-reliance).

Values are the reason why two people who support renewable energy can disagree vehemently on policy (positive versus negative reinforcement).

Understanding this is good news. Because identifying their values — the context that has them already supporting an issue — is your key to untangling any confusion about their stance on an issue. It is also your key to translating your cause into language that they will understand and resonate with in the future.

### Critical Questions

- Do you understand the values behind the behaviors you see others engaging in?
- Have you taken the time to get to know why they do what they do?

> **Practical Exercises**
>
> Identify the values behind an individual's eco-personality type. Begin to laser-focus your approach. Reference your earlier exercise identifying eco-personality types.
> - Have you heard them use any of the value words related to their eco-personality type when discussing their passion?
> - What would you guess their underlying values are related to their cause?
> - Ask them. Check for accuracy. Say, "It really seems like you value [x], is that true?" Truly listen to their response.
> - Once you've identified their underlying values behind their eco-personality type, look into your heart again and find a way to support them in their passion without compromising your own integrity. What would that look like?
> - When the time comes to share your own cause and passion, make sure that every time you discuss it with them, you frame it in language they will understand and resonate with.

## Mirroring

How do you get rapport with just about anybody, in the shortest period of time, in the most fulfilling way?

Tony Robbins is famous for saying, "The obvious way to start with is really caring. There is no faking sincerity. But there are some skill sets also that will cause people to feel connected to you in a matter of minutes and also cause you to feel connected to other people who maybe normally you wouldn't have felt that way with."

Most people think that asking questions is how you build rapport. It's not. Questions are simply tools you can use to learn what will build rapport – having something in common. Everything discussed in this book has been about helping you find your shared humanity with those you disagree with.

You may have noticed that questions can only give you tidbits of information about a person. You may have to ask a tiring amount of questions before you find that thing you do have in common.

- Where are you from? Farm, suburbs, city.
- What do you do? Job, sports, hobbies, volunteering.
- Who do you know? Family, friends, business networks.
- What do you like? Pop culture, sub-culture, counter-culture.

Asking all of these questions can feel like an interview and create an awkward energy. Words don't always work.

Body language and learning styles are critical. Since people naturally communicate in the way they learn, you can take cues from their communication style to infer their learning style.

Milton Erikson, a world-renowned hypnotherapist in the '60s and '70s, was obsessed with the power of the unconscious mind. He was famous for getting results when years of other treatments and thousands of dollars did not work.

His secret was matching and mirroring his patients' body language and communication style to immediately build rapport. Specifically, he matched aspects of their voice (tone, speed, pitch) and mirrored their body language (positioning).

People take in information with five senses. These are our major styles of learning and communication: visual (eyes/seeing), auditory (ears/hearing), kinesthetic (skin/touch), olfactory (nose/smell), and gustatory (mouth/taste).

Three of these styles are always helpful in influencing others – visual, auditory, and kinesthetic. You shouldn't always go straight for the lick or sniff.

Besides being mostly harmless, sight, sound, and touch are literally hard-wired into your nervous system.

This means that body language provides very effective cues to read from others and mirror/match back to them.

Communication styles are a bit more intuitive. So, we'll go into each one next.

### Critical Questions

- What body language is the individual you want to influence displaying when you approach them? Are they sitting or standing? Leaning forward or back? Arms or legs crossed? Standing close or at a comfortable distance? Strong eye contact?

### Visual

Travis Langen is a visionary sustainability education leader, and was my director at the Catalina Environmental Leadership Program for two years. He would lead us out to the garden area during staff training and begin his sessions. It never failed. The man could not stay in one place.

He would reference the nursery in the distance, then shout, "You need to see this! Follow me." He would begin marching around the garden, pointing at things, waving his arms in grand gestures, and speaking rapidly with loud excitement. When he discussed his vision for a rehab project, out came his tattered sketch book. He would huddle us all around to see the beautiful drawings, then just as quickly be up pacing in circles drawing a map of the new design with his steps. It was hilarious! And incredibly effective for the staff who were visual learners, like myself.

When I wanted to develop a new program to teach students how new, innovative companies were adopting sustainability practices, Travis was skeptical. So, I turned it into a flash card game with images of products kids could see and recognize on the front. On the back was a brief description of how each product was made — and how that was better for the environment. Then, I was energetic and excited when I presented it to him — gesturing to show him what a lesson would look like in action.

The activity was approved.

### Critical Questions

- Is the person you are trying to influence a visual learner?
- Do they talk a little louder, faster, and more intensely than you do?
- Are they gesturing with their hands to help construct an image of what they are trying to convey?
- Do they say things like, "Look at this," "Can you see?" or "Let me show you"?

### Auditory

My senior vice president last year requested brief one-page summaries of our big sustainability goals and vision for the future. She needed it for our annual strategic planning session. I wasn't sure what to do. She had images, descriptions, spreadsheets, etc. And I finally realized that the most value we got out of our interactions was always in our monthly one-on-ones. She would just listen and talk and discuss. Questions and answers. Rarely anything more. And I always left feeling like we had made real headway in understanding each other.

So, I bought some inexpensive software and built three short and simple videos — one for each big goal in our vision. Nothing flashy. And I used a calm, nicely paced voice-over for each one that walked through the basics. She loved it! She said, "These were great. I felt like I really understood them, compared to the one-pagers. These are just what we need." It was a success.

### Critical Questions

- Is the person you are trying to influence an auditory learner?
- Do they talk a little slower, with a calm, smooth rhythm?
- Do they gesture slowly, in rhythm with their voice, not so much to paint a picture?
- Do they say things like, "Listen," "I hear you," or "That clicks for me"?

## Kinesthetic

My direct supervisor was possibly my favorite boss ever. He's an engineer who has field experience, management experience, and sales experience. He is also a "feeler." Every week in our one-on-ones, we talk about travel plans. He grabs his computer monitor, pushes it around so I can see it, opens up Google Maps, and starts pointing and dragging all over the place. When we discuss ideas, he sits back and ponders what I'm sharing. He's slow to answer, always with a quiet thoughtfulness. Often, he grins and grabs a pen and one-sided paper from his bin, scratching out a simple diagram of what he thinks we should be doing. And he's quick to give a firm handshake or a pat on the back.

So, when I wanted to try a new LED light for a flag pole application, first I brought in a sample. Then I crunched the numbers and printed graphs and pie charts he could red-line on paper. Next, we hopped in the car and visited a store. Some of his best advice was to "let people see and touch what it is you want them to adopt." At our store, I had our vendor install the new LED lights next to the metal halide version with a toggle switch. We drove out at night and stood back as the switch toggled back and forth between the two lighting options. He was convinced.

### Critical Questions

- Is the person you are trying to influence a kinesthetic learner?
- Do they talk less, usually quietly, and show by example more?
- Do they grab for things to demonstrate their point?
- Do they say things like, "I need a more concrete example," "It doesn't feel right," or "I need a better sense of this"?

**Practical Exercises**

Mirror and match the individual you are trying to influence. Identify their body language and dominant learning style. Begin to laser-focus your approach by seeing where some major differences exist between you. Minimize those differences by adapting some (not all) of your body language and communication style to mirror their own.
- Pay attention to the body language of the person. Choose one aspect of their body language that is most unlike your own. Could that be a sign that you are in a different mood or frame of mind?
- Consider adapting your posture, lean, intensity, etc. to more closely mirror their own state. See what happens.
- Pay attention to the learning style of the individual. Choose one aspect of their dominant communication style that is most unlike your own. Could that be a sign that you are not connecting when discussing issues that you care about?
- The key difference between kinesthetic and visual is action. A visual learner might be happy seeing a photo of the LED lighting installed. A kinesthetic learner would need to go see it and touch it for themselves. A visual learner also tends to be a louder/faster talker.
- Consider adapting your volume or pace when speaking. Consider how your gestures or phrasing might more closely mirror their own style. See what happens if you try to find additional ways to align your communication with their learning style.

## Credible Sources

When I see someone in another country unwilling to attempt to speak the language, I usually view them as arrogant. I assume they are only focused on what they need and want, expecting everyone else to adapt to them.

Learning styles and communication styles are like separate countries. If you notice how someone prefers to learn and share, and you actually care about them, it's a sign of respect to at least attempt to mirror and match their preferred methods.

Similar to how we naturally communicate in the way we learn best, we also naturally share sources of information that we ourselves find credible. When asking individuals about their own passions, pay attention to what sources they use to share with you what they care about. If someone sends you a scientific article from a right-wing major news site, don't send them back an editorial post from an obscure left-wing blog. There will be less receptivity. Do your research, and work hard at it. Invest some of your time and give it some forethought.

A great response would be to send a "Thank you" for the article. Find and share at least one thing you agreed with to show that you read what they sent. If you must, send back an article by the exact same author contradicting themselves in the past or adding a more accurate viewpoint to what may have been taken out of context.

That's not always possible, but you get my point. If they share a video, magazine, newspaper, link to a website, etc. then send them the same next time. Look for a similar author, news site, or geographic region. Something similar has got to be available.

People are constantly showing you what they desperately seek in return. If you are thoughtful enough to pay attention, they are handing you your winning game plan on a silver platter. Care enough to take notes.

The critic in you may say, "I'm not a going to be a phony!"

No one is asking you to be fake. I'm asking you to be respectful of how people learn, communicate, and share. Do so in a way that honors their process. Luckily for you, this also will produce more of the results you are looking for.

### Critical Questions

- What sources does the person you are trying to influence send you when sharing about their passions?

**Practical Exercises**

Mirror and match the sources of information shared with you by the individual you are trying to influence. Identify their favorite sources of information – authors, publications, websites, news stations, groups, etc. Begin to laser-focus your approach by seeing where some major differences exist between you. Minimize those differences by adapting some (not all) of your sources to mirror their own and build credibility.
- Pay attention to the sources of information this individual sends you. Choose one aspect of their idea of credible sources that is most unlike your own. Could that be a sign that your messages are not being considered based on their origin?
- Consider adapting your arsenal of facts, figures, ideas and examples to more closely mirror their own perspective on credible sources. See what happens.

**Additional Resources**

- **The Environmental Case** (book) by Judith Layzer
- **The New Rules of Green Marketing** (book) by Jacquelyn Ottman
- **Influence** (book) by Robert Cialdini
- **Sway** (book) by Ori Brafman
- **Nudge** (book) by Richard Thaler

# SUMMARY

*"Be who God meant you to be, and you will set the world on fire."*
~ Catherine of Siena

Consider reading this book a second or third time through. In so doing, return to those memories from when you had already successfully used the concepts discussed in these pages. Celebrate your wins, no matter how large or small. Millions of us are playing the same advocacy game together, although it can sometimes feel lonely. We are all experiencing similar struggles and still making incredible things happen.

You made it to the end of this book because you care. Your life is about something more than yourself. And because of that reality, you are bound to come up against roadblocks and speed bumps along your journey.

Conflict is inevitable. Opposition is unavoidable. Strong emotions are highly probable. It's all a part of your path as a human being who is up to something big in life.

Don't burn out. Don't give in. If you've already quit, this little book is your ticket back into the game.

I know what it feels like, and so do thousands of other sustainability champions just like you. We all struggle. But you don't have to stay stuck.

You can be free from the vicious cycle of frustration and burn-out – the exhaustion of advocacy.

I know because it happened to me. I was burnt out. I was suppressing, then reacting to, my own emotions because I believed I needed to in order to be successful.

It doesn't work.

There are plenty of myths and limiting beliefs that are commonplace in our field. And now that you've seen them for what they are – and have been offered a host of new strategies and tools to approach your passion – you can completely transform your ability to successfully be the change you want see in the world.

The world needs it. The world needs you. Social and environmental issues aren't going to solve themselves.

You never again need to feel paralyzed when confronted with the problems we face as one global family. When others deny or dismiss true problems that exist, you can see past media and politics. You can see past the exaggeration and sensationalism. You can act when others are uncertain.

## Beyond Facts

Facts, delivered poorly, are considered facts by few.

You have enough facts – data, science, and numbers. If you hold and understand the facts, what you need is a healthy dose of influence. You are in a select group that is actually capable of saving society and the planet. And it's your responsibility to get better at talking to those on the other side of the fence.

Now, you can supplement your facts with just the right amount of emotional intelligence and psychology to cause behavior change. You can be more aware of your own emotional state and leverage those feelings in healthy and productive ways. You can recognize the stages of influence others are going through and apply the appropriate strategies to help them through their process. You can identify and prioritize the groups to target when working on any campaign. And you can master the art and science of persuasion to influence individuals in your life and community who make decisions that affect others around them. That is what this book provides you.

## Take It from Me

If you'll accept it, I've offered the only thing I know– well over a decade's worth of struggles and experience to learn from. It's all organized into a simple and easy-to-understand framework based on emotional intelligence research and psychology. You've heard stories from my own successes and failures as a frustrated introvert, a book worm turned sustainability consultant, speaker and coach.

I struggled often. But I was fortunate enough to interview over 200 leaders about what worked for them. I was lucky to meet new heroes like Hunter Lovins, Ray Anderson, Bob Willard, and Simran Sethi who set me on the path that was much more stress-free. That path resulted in more meaningful results. I was able to leverage my emotions, avoid burnout, and start influencing anyone.

Now, you can do the same. In all likelihood, you will take this farther than I ever could. And nothing would make me happier.

## What's Next?

You now have the insight and inspiration you've been looking for. Dozens of new approaches to championing sustainability are now at your service. You can tailor the way you speak, the way you write, and the way you approach problems to get the results you want.

You can take on more than one issue at a time. You can customize a unique and stage-appropriate strategy every time.

You now understand and can start to recognize that individuals you speak to have their own perspective – around which you can frame your communications. No more of the right idea at the wrong time. No more one-size-fits-all. No more wasted time and energy. No more giving away your power to people you don't need to influence.

You can learn from my mistakes, and achieve your own goals even faster.

## Use Your New Skill Set

I can't imagine that you would put down this book and not use what you just read.

I can't imagine that you would keep doing things the same way, or be unwilling to try something new, if any of your past efforts have proven frustrating or unfruitful.

But if you feel that way, I have one request. Reach out to me. Email me. Call me. Comment on my blog. Get onto my Facebook page and talk to others who follow me. I will connect you with a community of activists that are up to the things you are.

Don't just pick up another book and not apply anything you've heard here. Take new action. Give something new a shot. I failed often, but failure is sometimes the best teacher. It's called experience.

Willpower alone will fade over time if you continue to come up short. You don't have a good reason to become cynical any more – about the world, your co-workers and bosses, or even your own ability to make a difference. If you have damaged relationships, you can repair them. If you are growing frustrated with those you believe should change, you can shift your approach today.

Just as I contemplated several times, if you don't try these new approaches, you may eventually quit. And no one wants that to happen.

## My Personal Guarantee

If you didn't take away one thing from this book, email me and share your story so we can update the book to cover your unique situation.

This little book can completely shift how you look at making a difference. It can make the world feel like a simpler place. You can start to notice things you've never noticed, which are the keys to your success.

Continue to come back to the new perspectives in these short chapters. You can practice influence techniques that seem effortless in comparison to what you're accustomed to. You can work less and accomplish more. You can be happier, have more energy, and build relationships that you never thought possible. Your circle of influence can expand. Your confidence can soar. You can tackle larger and larger issues wherever you feel called to contribute.

You can build larger and larger coalitions in your community to implement change.

And you can share these simple strategies with more change agents just like you. You can help others wake up to what's possible and change the world together. Thanks to you, we will be able to live in a world that is happier, healthier, and more sustainable for all.

## One Million Minds

Close your eyes and visualize with me one more time.

Envision a world where passion and caring are constantly being translated into powerful action. Picture socially- and environmentally-conscious people around the world having high-impact conversations that produce amazing results in their communities.

Imagine yourself and twenty other visionary leaders in your city. See them having several conversations throughout their day – on the phone, around the table, in a meeting, at a coffee shop, in front of a crowd – and people are listening. The message is getting through. Those who you expect to argue, shut down, or turn off are showing interest. Those from whom you expect mild support are making commitments and taking action. And the visionary leaders – that's you – are generating meaningful change more rapidly than they ever thought possible.

I hope you're smiling. I am, just writing it.

I invite you to join me and thousands of other change agents in this One Million Minds campaign.

It's my vision that – together – we can help one million passionate people around the world leverage their emotions, avoid burnout, and influence anyone.

This is sure to move, inspire, and transform our communities, one by one, creating a tipping point for the planet. Together, I believe we can do that – One Million Minds strong.

If you bought the print version of this book, you've already contributed by donating $1 to two organizations ensuring that the next generation understands sustainability: Net Impact and AASHE (Association for the Advancement of Sustainability in Higher Education). These two organizations are helping our next generation participate in solving the critical social and environmental issues of this generation.

You read this far. You have what it takes, and more.

I applaud you. I respect you. Thank you for what you're up to in life. The world needs more people just like you.

This is your new playbook. Use it. Adapt it. Make it your own. Make the difference you always believed you could. And share your stories with the world.

# ABOUT THE AUTHOR

Today, Adam Hammes is an independent sustainability consultant in Des Moines, Iowa, where he helps businesses tackle sustainability – from local restaurant chains to international media companies. He staffs the Iowa Sustainable Business Forum and sits on the Greater Des Moines Partnership's Sustainability Committee and the Solidarity Microfinance Committee. He coaches sustainability professionals around the world and speaks at conferences on stress-free sustainability.

Adam grew up in a rural, conservative farm community and struggled expressing his own environmental views. In college, he led outdoor adventure trips, earned his minor in environmental studies and a certificate in global health. After graduation, he traveled the world as an environmental educator and leadership trainer, living and working in seven countries on four continents. He earned his MBA, LEED-AP (BD+C), and LCA Manager Certificate. He trained with The Natural Step USA: Level 1 & 2 and with the Wilderness Stewardship Program.

In 2008, Adam founded a grassroots sustainability non-profit called Urban Ambassadors. Through their work, he spearheaded several projects, including: school gardens, a green CEO speaker series, a transportation photo shoot, pop-up parks in Park(ing) Day spaces downtown, an annual conference that brought together the local food and hunger fighting communities, and a group micro-lending program for women in poverty modeled after Grameen Bank.

In 2010, Adam became the corporate manager of sustainability for Kum & Go, a convenience store chain with $3 billion in revenue. He helped them institutionalize green building, the only convenience store chain in the world certified in the LEED Volume Program. When he left after three and a half years, they had gone from two to over eighty LEED-certified locations, and from zero to over one hundred locations having at-the-pump recycling for customers.

Adam has lived car-less for years in the city. He loves to read, write, meditate, recreate outdoors, travel, and play guitar. Today, he lives two hours from his parents' farm and loves to visit and spend time with his family and brother.

## FEEDBACK

Thank you for purchasing this book.

I truly appreciate your thoughts and feelings, and would love hearing what you have to say about making this book and my other work better so it can reach more people and make a difference in their life. My ego can take it.

Please leave the world an honest and helpful review on Amazon, too. It is the lifeblood of any good book.

I actually need (need, need, need!) your input to make any future work I do even more impactful, so we can reach our vision of One Million Minds.

Gratefully, Adam
February 26, 2015

## MORE RESOURCES

Visit www.eco-fluence.com and sign up for free email training. You can also contact Adam about your own passions if you need professional coaching or a speaker for an event.

## ONE MILLION MINDS

Thank you! If you purchased a print copy of this book, you just donated $1 each to two amazing organizations: Net Impact and the Association for the Advancement of Sustainability in Higher Education (AASHE). These two organizations are helping emerging leaders participate in solving the critical social and environmental issues of this generation.

You joined me and thousands of other change agents in this *One Million Minds* campaign. It's my vision that – together – we can help one million passionate people around the world leverage their emotions, avoid burnout, and influence anyone. This is sure to move, inspire, and transform our communities, one by one, creating a tipping point for the planet. Together, I believe we can do that – *One Million Minds* strong. Let your friends know about this book.

## NET IMPACT

Net Impact is a leading nonprofit that empowers a new generation to change the world. The problems our world faces are huge, from poverty to climate change to global health epidemics. What if we could mobilize more people to dedicate more time on the job to making an impact? We believe this shift is essential to creating a more sustainable world.

Every day, Net Impact helps students and professionals to drive social and environmental change on campus and throughout their careers. We provide the network and resources to inspire emerging leaders to build successful "impact careers," either by working in jobs dedicated to change or by bringing a social and environmental lens to traditional business roles.

The Net Impact community is more than 60,000 leaders from 300-plus volunteer-led chapters across the globe, working for a more sustainable future. Together, we make a net impact that transforms our lives, our organizations, and the world.

Learn more. Visit www.netimpact.org

AASHE is an independent 501(c)(3) helping to create a brighter future of opportunity for all by advancing sustainability in higher education. By creating a diverse community engaged in sharing ideas and promising practices, AASHE provides administrators, faculty, staff and students, as well as the business that serve them, with: thought leadership and essential knowledge resources; outstanding opportunities for professional development; and a unique framework for demonstrating the value and competitive edge created by sustainability initiatives.

AASHE defines sustainability in an inclusive way, encompassing human and ecological health, social justice, secure livelihoods, and a better world for all generations.

Learn more. Visit www.aashe.org